B-52G/H Stratofortr

Written by Kenneth P. Katz

In Action®

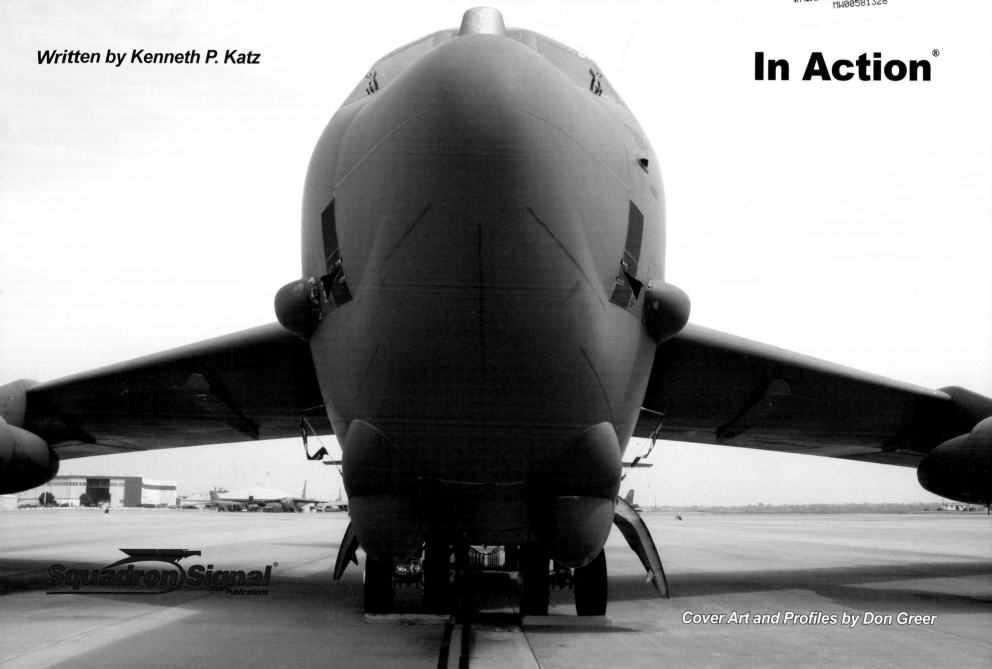

Squadron Signal® Publications

Cover Art and Profiles by Don Greer

(Front Cover) B-52H 60-0022 carries four GAM-87 Skybolt missiles.

(Back Cover) On the first mission of the "Shock and Awe" phase of Operation Iraqi Freedom on 21 March 2003, B-52H 60-0060 *Iron Butterfly* (call sign "Dogleg 25"/"Ratlr 82") leads the 23rd Expeditionary Bomb Squadron, 457th Air Expeditionary Group, from its base at RAF Fairford in the United Kingdom toward targets in Iraq. The sortie duration was 16.1 hours, and the crew was pilot Capt. Jason D. Horton, co-pilot 1st Lt. Douglas C. Farley, radar navigator Capt. Patrick S. McDonald, navigator 2nd Lt. Daniel S. Lambert, and electronic warfare officer Capt. Thomas H. Dillion. During the mission, *Iron Butterfly* launched all eight of its missiles, primarily against targets in the Baghdad area.

Don Greer 2007

2

About the In Action® Series

In Action® books, despite the title of the genre, are books that trace the development of a single type of aircraft, armored vehicle, or ship from prototype to the final production variant. Experimental or "one-off" variants can also be included. Our first *In Action®* book was printed in 1971.

Hardcover ISBN 978-0-89747-688-1
Softcover ISBN 978-0-89747-687-4

www.SquadronSignalPublications.com

 Proudly printed in the U.S.A.
Copyright 2012 Squadron/Signal Publications
1115 Crowley Drive, Carrollton, TX 75006-1312 U.S.A.

Military/Combat Photographs and Snapshots

If you have any photos of aircraft, armor, soldiers, or ships of any nation, particularly wartime snapshots, why not share them with us and help make Squadron/Signal's books all the more interesting and complete in the future? Any photograph sent to us will be copied and returned. Electronic images are preferred. The donor will be fully credited for any photos used. Please send them to:

Squadron/Signal Publications
1115 Crowley Drive
Carrollton, TX 75006-1312 U.S.A.

(Title Page) A B-52H of the 2nd Bomb Wing awaits its next mission at its home base of Barksdale AFB. Carrying equipment and weapons that were not even imagined when it was built, the B-52H soldiers on. (Author)

Acknowledgments

The author appreciates the support given by the personnel of Air Force Public Affairs, Air Combat Command headquarters, 2nd Bomb Wing, 5th Bomb Wing, 917th Wing, 31st Test and Evaluation Squadron, 49th Test and Evaluation Squadron, Aerospace Maintenance and Regeneration Center, Air Armament Center, Air Force Flight Test Center, NASA Dryden Flight Research Center, Northrop Grumman, Oklahoma City Air Logistics Center, John W. Ramsay Research Library of the New England Air Museum, Raytheon Missile Systems, and Lockheed Martin. The 21st Space Wing provided aerospace physiology training to the author in preparation for his B-52H flight. Many individuals provided interviews. Photographs are credited in their captions. Photographs credited to Lockheed Martin and Raytheon were used with permission.

B-52H 61-0035 cruises at high altitude on a training mission. This aircraft is marked with the MT tail code of the 5th Bomb Wing (BW) at Minot AFB and the black and red checkerboard tail stripe of the 69th Bomb Squadron (BS), which is assigned to the 5th BW. (Staff Sgt. Andy M. Kin / USAF)

More than any other weapon system, the legendary Boeing B-52 Stratofortress is the embodiment of American military power in the popular imagination. The B-52 was the workhorse of the Strategic Air Command (SAC) in its nuclear deterrent role, the most important mission during the Cold War. Perhaps the most impressive aspect of the B-52 has been its longevity. The B-52 first flew in 1952 and entered operational service with the U.S. Air Force in 1955. Boeing delivered the last B-52 in 1962. Five decades later, the B-52 remains in front-line service, most recently taking part in combat over Afghanistan and Iraq. Even more amazingly, current plans are for the B-52 to remain in service until 2040. It is as if the Wright Flyer conducted combat missions in World War II and then remained in service through the end of the Cold War.

The earlier Boeing B-47 bomber laid the technological foundation for the B-52. The B-47 Stratojet was an extraordinary leap in aircraft design. Merely a few years later in design than the propeller-driven bombers of World War II, the B-47 featured swept wings, turbojet engines suspended in pods beneath the wings, aerial refueling capability, and a yaw damper stability augmentation system. The B-47 was not just a highly capable bomber; it has also defined the basic configuration for most large subsonic jet aircraft to this day. The basic layout of the B-52 was designed by Boeing engineers Ed Wells and George Schairer in 1948. Much larger than the B-47, the B-52 had eight Pratt & Whitney J57 turbojet engines instead of the six J47 turbojets of the B-47. The combination of the large airframe, advanced J57 engines, and aerial refueling achieved the "Holy Grail" of aircraft design for that era, a heavy bomber with intercontinental range and high speed.

The B-52 was shaped around its bomb bay. To prevent the aircraft from losing control because of the massive shift in weight when a weapon was released, the bomb bay had to be located at the B-52's center of gravity. This meant that the wing box structure had to be over the bomb bay, which resulted in a high wing configuration. The landing gear could not be mounted on the high wing, so the B-52 had a quadricycle landing gear design with main landing gears ahead of and behind the bomb bay. In turn, the quadricycle landing gears needed to be supplemented by outrigger landing gear on the wing tips to prevent the tips from dragging on the ground when heavy with fuel. The quadricycle and outrigger landing gear combination prevented the B-52 from using the conventional method of taking off and landing in a crosswind by lowering the upwind wing. Instead, the B-52 had an ingenious crosswind crab landing-gear design.

The first prototype B-52, the XB-52, rolled out of the Boeing plant in Seattle, Washington, in 1951, and the second prototype, the YB-52, made the first flight on 15 April 1952. These two aircraft were followed by the B-52A, which replaced the tandem cockpit and bubble canopy of the XB-52 and YB-52 with a conventional bomber cockpit

The B-47 pioneered the basic elements of the aerodynamic design later used by the B-52: swept wings and podded jet engines. There was a strong family resemblance between the B-47 and the much larger B-52. (USAF)

The XB-52 and YB-52 were the prototypes for the 744 Stratofortresses that were eventually built. The Pratt & Whitney J57 engine made the B-52 possible, and the B-52 had eight of these engines arranged in four pairs (USAF)

having the two pilots sitting side by side and increased the maximum gross weight to 420,000 pounds from the 405,000 pounds of the XB-52 and YB-52. Only three B-52A aircraft were built, and they were used for testing and development, never entering service with operational bomber squadrons. The B-52B and its reconnaissance version, the RB-52B, were the first to enter operational service, with B-52B 52-8711 being delivered to the 93rd Bombardment Wing (BMW), Castle AFB, on 29 July 1955.

The maximum gross weight of the B-52C increased to 450,000 pounds, with that model having underwing 3,000-gallon fuel tanks. B-52 output really hit its stride with the B-52D, the production of which was split between the Boeing factories in Seattle and Wichita. All earlier B-52s had only been built in Seattle. Eventually the B-52D fleet received the "Big Belly" modification to carry up to 108 conventional bombs, which made it the mainstay of the Arc Light and Linebacker raids during the Vietnam War.

Externally, the B-52E was indistinguishable from the B-52D except for paint and markings, but internally it gained the AN/ASQ-38 bombing and navigation system, which heralded the shift from high-altitude to low-altitude tactics for penetrating Soviet airspace. The B-52F introduced J57-P-43W engines with higher thrust and a new electrical generation system that was more powerful, more reliable and safer. The B-52F was the last model to have its production in both Seattle and Wichita. It was also the first model of B-52 to see combat in Vietnam, although it was soon replaced by the B-52Ds with the Big Belly modification. Boeing delivered the last B-52F in 1959.

By this time, SAC had achieved a truly awesome and unprecedented level of capability, with over a thousand B-47 and B-52 bombers, abundant thermonuclear weapons, hundreds of KC-97 and KC-135 tankers, and a global command, control and communications capability. With much of its force on alert, SAC could have obliterated the Soviet Union, China, and every other Communist country within 24 hours.

B-52A 52-003 was modified to become the NB-52A mothership for the X-15. Starting with the B-52A, the B-47-style tandem cockpit of the XB-52 and YB-52 were changed to a conventional cockpit with the pilot and co-pilot sitting side by side. (NASA Dryden Flight Research Center)

B-52E 56-631 is the first Seattle-built B-52E. With its AN/ASQ-38 bombing and navigation system, the B-52E signaled the shift from high-altitude to low-altitude flight to avoid Soviet air defenses. (USAF)

B-52F 57-0156 of the 436th Bombardment Squadron (BMS), 4238th Strategic Wing, was at Barksdale AFB, Louisiana, in the early 1960s. The B-52 fleet of the era had aluminized paint on the upper surfaces. The white undersides were intended to reflect the intense heat of thermonuclear explosions. The blue Strategic Air Command (SAC) sash was painted on both sides of the nose. (USAF)

B-52G

To fill the gap between the B-52 and a planned new generation of supersonic bombers, Boeing briefed the USAF on a significantly improved B-52 in March 1956. Essentially a second-generation B-52, the USAF designated the new model the B-52G.

The B-52G retained the engines and most of the avionics and systems of the B-52F. A variety of changes to the airframe structure reduced weight. The structure used a new aluminum alloy that was lighter and stronger. The new vertical stabilizer was the most distinctive change, being almost eight feet shorter than the fin on the earlier models. In the wings, integral fuel tanks replaced bladders. With the extra internal fuel capacity, 700-gallon fuel tanks on the wing tips replaced the 3,000-gallon tip tanks of the earlier models. The ailerons were deleted and all lateral control was done with spoilers. A one-piece nose radome for the navigation radar replaced the earlier two-piece radome. The gunner operated the new AN/ASG-15 defensive fire control system for the tail guns, remotely from the main crew compartment, no longer needing a separate pressurized compartment in the tail. Besides the addition of the gunner crew station, the crew compartment was redesigned for increased comfort. Together, all these changes resulted in a higher fuel capacity (6,425 more gallons than the B-52F), a higher maximum gross weight (488,000 pounds compared to 450,000 pounds for the B-52F) and a lighter empty weight (approximately 10,000 pounds less than the B-52F). The B-52G had about 1,000 miles longer range than the B-52F, with the exact improvement dependent on flight profile and bomb load. On 14 December 1960, a B-52G showed off its impressive range with a record-breaking unrefueled flight of 10,079 miles during Operation Long Jump.

The B-52G was also the first model of B-52 designed to carry missiles, although some older models were later retrofitted. The B-52G could carry four GAM-72 Quail decoys in its bomb bay and two GAM-77 Hound Dog nuclear-armed cruise missiles on underwing pylons. It also retained the ability to drop nuclear bombs.

The B-52G first flew in 1958 and entered service in 1959. The B-52G was the first model of B-52 to be built entirely in Wichita. Boeing delivered the last B-52G in 1961. With 193 aircraft manufactured, the B-52G was the most numerous model of the B-52.

For all its advances, the B-52G had deficiencies. The shorter vertical stabilizer and the lack of ailerons degraded the flying qualities of the B-52G compared to earlier models, especially when conducting aerial refueling, which is the most challenging task for B-52 pilots. The combination of the lighter structure, new aluminum alloy and turbulence during low-altitude flying caused extensive fatigue damage to the B-52G airframes after only a short time, in one instance causing the loss of B-52G 58-0187 due to catastrophic inflight structural failure with resulting fuel leaks and loss of control. The structural deficiencies necessitated a major program to upgrade the structure with a heavier but

B-52G 58-0212 shows the defensive armament configuration new to the B-52G. Earlier models had the gunner sitting in the tail. Starting with the B-52G, the gunner's crew station was in the cockpit and he operated the guns by remote control using the AN/ASG-15 fire control system. The radomes for the AN/ASG-15 search and track radars were located above the guns. (New England Air Museum collection)

B-52G 58-0194 of the 69th BMS, 42nd BMW is being prepared for flight at Loring AFB. Each pair of engines is connected to a starter cart. On alert, engine start was by pyrotechnic cartridges instead of starter carts. After the klaxon sounded, the alert crew was required to get to the bomber, start the engines and take off within a few minutes. (New England Air Museum collection)

B-52G (as delivered by Boeing)

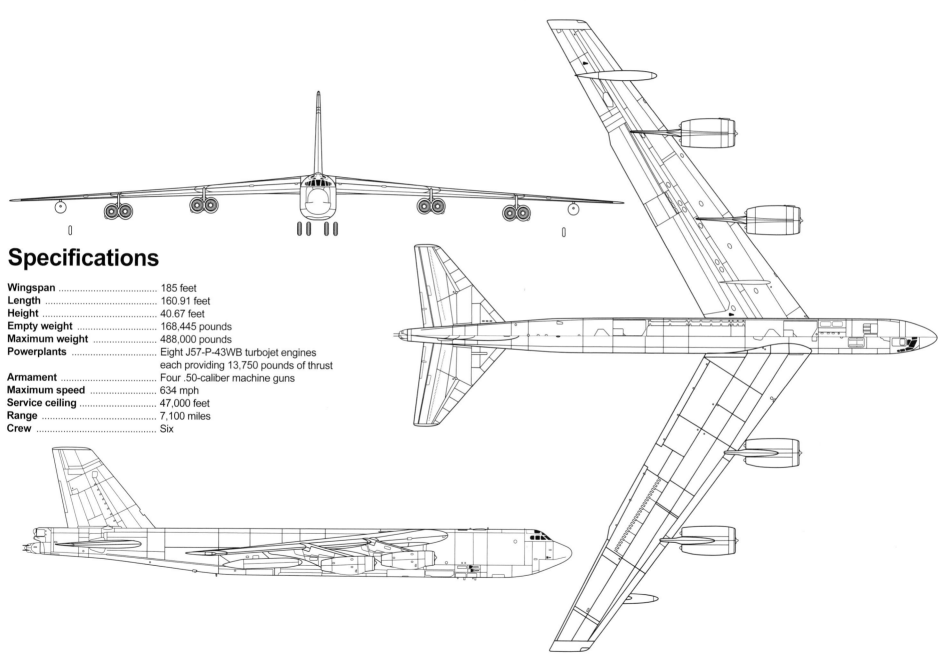

Specifications

Wingspan	185 feet
Length	160.91 feet
Height	40.67 feet
Empty weight	168,445 pounds
Maximum weight	488,000 pounds
Powerplants	Eight J57-P-43WB turbojet engines each providing 13,750 pounds of thrust
Armament	Four .50-caliber machine guns
Maximum speed	634 mph
Service ceiling	47,000 feet
Range	7,100 miles
Crew	Six

more damage-tolerant aluminum alloy. Even after the structural modifications, the B-52G proved to be less survivable after suffering combat damage during the Vietnam War than the older, heavier and stronger B-52D. Despite these problems, the performance advantage of the B-52G was undeniable.

With the B-52G being the most numerous model of B-52, and with second most numerous model, the B-52D, being used in the Vietnam War, the B-52G was the mainstay of SAC's nuclear deterrent during the Cold War. Starting in 1957, SAC put its bombers on ground alert. During the period 1960-1968, B-52s were also flying airborne alert with live nuclear weapons to guarantee that some portion for the force would not be destroyed on the ground during a surprise attack.

In the 1970s, the B-52G was modernized. The most important of these upgrades were the AN/ASQ-151 Electro-optical Viewing System (EVS), the AGM-69A Short Range Attack Missile (SRAM), and the Phase VI electronic countermeasures suite. These systems considerably altered the external appearance of the aircraft and degraded aerodynamic performance since they added various "lumps and bumps" to the previously clean B-52 airframe. More upgrades arrived in the 1980s. The aging AN/ASQ-38 bombing and navigation system was replaced by the digital AN/ASQ-176 Offensive Avionics System (OAS). OAS was not only more reliable and more accurate than the AN/ASQ-38, it also enabled the B-52G to align, target, and launch the AGM-86B Air Launched Cruise Missile (ALCM), which allowed the B-52 to remain a viable nuclear strike platform. Although all B-52Gs got OAS, only some aircraft were modified to carry ALCM.

The short tail of the B-52G was the most prominent difference between it and the preceding B-52 models. B-52G 57-6471 was the fourth B-52G built and is refueling from a KC-135A. (New England Air Museum collection)

B-52G 57-6518 is painted in the Strategic Integrated Operational Plan (SIOP) camouflage pattern and carries six AGM-69A Short Range Attack Missiles (SRAM) on each wing pylon. The combination of SRAM and having neither Electro-optical Viewing System (EVS) nor Phase VI electronic countermeasures (ECM) dates this picture to the early 1970s. (USAF)

B-52G 57-6498 wears the SIOP scheme, and has been modernized with EVS and the Phase VI electronic countermeasures suite. The orange tip tanks on this aircraft were modified to carry cameras in support of cruise missile testing. (USAF)

In the mid-1980s, the B-52 fleet began to be repainted in gray (FS36081) and green (FS 34086). B-52G 57-6479 sports the new colors. This was known as the Strategic paint scheme and was the predominant scheme during Operation Desert Storm. (USAF)

A B-52G refuels over the Red Sea during Operation Desert Storm in 1991. The aircraft was carrying bomb racks mounted on stub pylons suspended from the wings between the inboard engine pods and the fuselage. (Senior Airman Chris Putman / USAF)

B-52G 59-2594 *Memphis Belle III* had nose art that commemorated the famed B-17F 41-24485 *Memphis Belle,* the first American bomber to complete 25 combat missions with no crew losses during World War II. (Don S. Montgomery / USAF)

A tail turret with four remotely-controlled 0.50 caliber M3 machine guns comprised the defensive armament of the B-52G. The B-52G gunner sat forward with the rest of the crew, not in the tail as in earlier models. (Chief Master Sgt. Don Sutherland / USAF)

B-52H

The B-52G had hung the B-52F engines on a new airframe. The next model, the B-52H, completed the cycle of improvement by installing new engines on the B-52G airframe. Jet engine technology advanced rapidly during the 1950s, and for subsonic flight the turbofan was a major improvement over the turbojet. Compared to the Pratt & Whitney J57-P-43WB turbojet of the B-52G, the Pratt & Whitney TF33-P-3 turbofan produced more thrust and had 13% lower specific fuel consumption. With the new turbofan engines, the B-52H climbed faster and flew further than the B-52G. The B-52H was popular with USAF pilots, who gave it the nickname "Cadillac."

In a turbojet engine like the J57-P-43WB, all the airflow went through the compressor, then the combustion chamber, and finally the turbine stage and exhaust nozzle. In contrast, a turbofan like the TF33-P-3 had a fan in front of the compressor. Some of the airflow from the fan went through the compressor and then the combustion chamber, turbine, and nozzle. The rest of the airflow from the fan bypassed the engine core and was pushed out the back of the engine. Compared to turbojet, a turbofan had higher thrust at low speeds and higher efficiency, at the cost a larger frontal area (which caused more drag) and heavier weight. On 10-11 January 1962, a B-52H of the 525th BMS, 4136th Strategic Wing set a new record by flying 12,532 miles unrefueled from Kadena Air Base, Okinawa, to Torrejon Air Base, Spain.

The turbofans also allowed the elimination of the problematic water injection system used by the J57-P-43WB and earlier models of the J57. The fundamental flaw of the J57 was its low thrust at low speed, which meant that the B-52 required long runways when fully loaded and had marginal performance when an engine failed during takeoff. To provide more thrust on takeoff, the J57 used a water injection system during warm outside air temperature. The water injection system pumped demineralized water into the air inlet and diffuser section of each engine. As the water vaporized, it cooled the air in the engine and increased its density. The higher density equated to higher airflow though the engine and therefore higher thrust. The downside of this thrust augmentation was decreased safety, since the water injection system occasionally failed, leaving the pilot to handle a suddenly underpowered airplane with asymmetric thrust at a critical phase of flight. Also, loading and unloading the water as the weather changed was burdensome to SAC maintenance personnel.

The other significant change in the B-52H was the replacement of the quadruple 0.50-caliber machine guns in the tail turret and AN/ASG-15 defensive fire control system with a 20mm, six-barrel M61A1 gun and AN/ASG-21 defensive fire control system. Compared to the previous armament system, the 20mm cannon fired heavier, faster projectiles with three times the hitting power of 0.50-caliber bullets, at a higher rate

Compared to the B-52G, the B-52H could be identified by the bypass ducts of its TF33-P-3 turbofan engines and the six-barrel, 20mm cannon in the tail. The B-52H was the ultimate model of the B-52 Stratofortress. Its performance and range were superior to those of the B-52G. (USAF)

After 35 years in service, the B-52H had FS36081 Gunship Gray paint, EVS under the nose, Phase VI electronic countermeasures antennas and radomes, an extended tail "stinger" also for the Phase VI suite, and no more tail gun. (Master Sgt. Michael A. Kaplan / USAF)

B-52H (modernized configuration as of 2007)

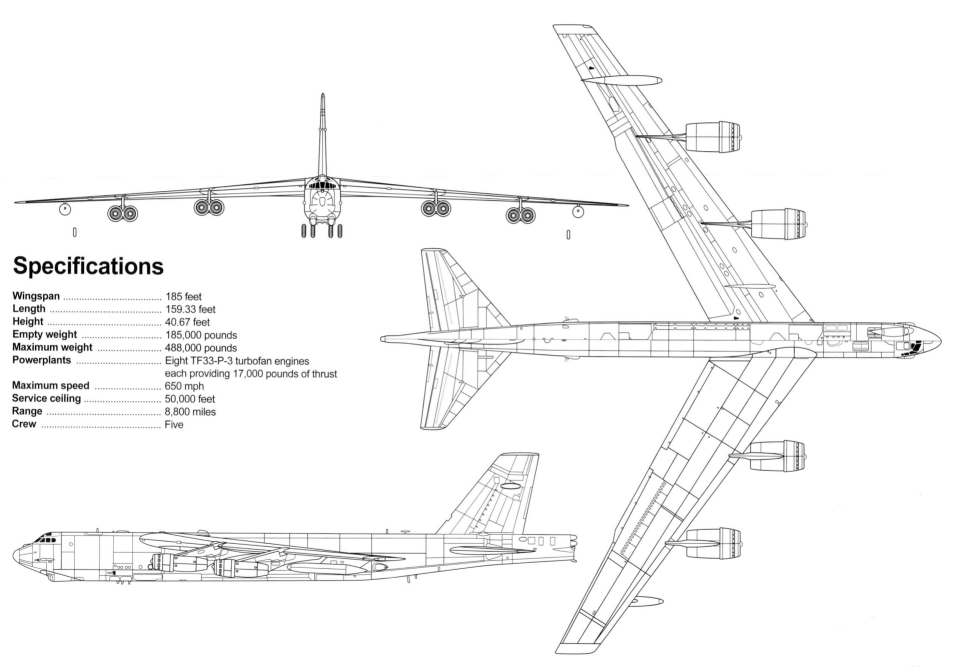

Specifications

Wingspan	185 feet
Length	159.33 feet
Height	40.67 feet
Empty weight	185,000 pounds
Maximum weight	488,000 pounds
Powerplants	Eight TF33-P-3 turbofan engines each providing 17,000 pounds of thrust
Maximum speed	650 mph
Service ceiling	50,000 feet
Range	8,800 miles
Crew	Five

of fire. The B-52H had several minor enhancements, including a rest bunk in the crew compartment and an improved interphone communications system.

The B-52H was sufficiently improved over the B-52G to justify acquisition of one final model of the B-52. By the late 1950s, USAF was focused on the supersonic B-70 as its bomber of the future, and it regarded the B-52H as an interim aircraft. Yet, as this book is being written in 2012 the "interim" B-52H has been flying for 50 years, with several more decades of service planned, and the lone surviving B-70 has been a museum exhibit since 1969.

The Douglas GAM-87 Skybolt air-launched ballistic missile was the intended offensive armament of the B-52H. The B-52H carried four missiles. After the cancellation of the Skybolt program in 1962, the B-52H had the same armament options as the B-52G: Hound Dog, Quail, and nuclear bombs.

The B-52H Stratofortress first flew in 1961. Later that year it entered operational service with SAC, the first unit equipped with the aircraft being the 524th BMS, 379th BMW. Boeing built all 102 B-52H aircraft in Wichita, Kansas. The last B-52H was delivered in 1962, completing a total B-52 production run of 744 aircraft.

Unlike the B-52G, the B-52H did not see combat in either Vietnam or Operation Desert Storm. During those conflicts, the B-52H fleet remained on alert with nuclear weapons. In general, the B-52H followed the same modernization path as the B-52G in the 1970s and 1980s: EVS, SRAM, Phase VI electronic countermeasures suite, OAS, and ALCM.

B-52H 60-0052 of the 96th BS, 2nd BW turns towards the initial point to deliver a GBU-12 Paveway II laser-guided bomb during a Combat Hammer operational test. This aircraft had the LA tail code of the 2nd BW and the red tail band of the 96th BS. (Samuel King Jr. / USAF)

B-52H 60-0009 of the 23rd BS, 5th BW takes off from Minot AFB. Its enormous Fowler flaps are extended, which increase the area and camber of the wing for increased lift at low speeds. (Senior Airman Araceli Alarcon / USAF)

Mechanics have removed the cowling from the #3 engine of this aircraft for maintenance. The prominent bypass ducts for the TF33-P-3 fan airflow were the primary distinguishing feature of the B-52H. (Author)

Augmenting the airbrakes and wheel brakes, a 44-foot diameter drag chute provided deceleration during the landing roll. The parachute was installed in a compartment aft of the rudder on the top of the tail section of the fuselage. (Staff Sgt. Tia Wilson / USAF)

B-52H 60-0012 *Heavy Hauler* of the 69th BS, 5th BW illustrates a modernized B-52H with the Phase VI electronics countermeasures suite radomes and EVS sensors turrets. (Senior Airman Benjamin Stratton / USAF)

A B-52H taxies out during a rapid-launch scenario. The Forward-Looking Infrared (FLIR) sensor (right EVS turret, as viewed from the cockpit) is exposed. The STV sensor is in the stowed position. (Senior Airman Kelly Timney / USAF)

The aircraft commander/pilot sat in the forward left seat and the copilot sat in the right front seat. Both crew positions had upward-firing ejection seats. (Master Sgt. Val Gempis / USAF)

Pilot visibility was adequate although nothing like that on a fighter with bubble canopy. The windows above the windshield were essential for air refueling. (Staff Sgt. Andy M. Kin / USAF)

The pilot used his right hand to manipulate the eight throttles, with eight sets of engine instruments forward of the throttle quadrant. The pilot's EVS monitor to the left of the engine instruments displayed FLIR and STV sensor video as well as terrain avoidance data. (Staff Sgt. Christopher Boitz / USAF)

The radar navigator (left) and the navigator (right) sat in downward-firing ejection seats in lower level of the crew compartment, facing forward. Each crew station had OAS controls and two monochrome OAS multifunction displays. (Master Sgt. Lance Cheung, USAF)

The ultimate purpose of every system on the B-52 and every Airman in an operational unit was to put weapons on targets. The B-52H could carry an extraordinary quantity and variety of weapons. (Tech. Sgt. Robert Horstman / USAF)

Military strategy during the Eisenhower administration was based on "massive retaliation" with nuclear weapons. All B-52s had been designed to carry 27 Mk 82 500-pound bombs or M117 750-pound bombs internally in their bomb bays, but SAC doctrine at the time of their delivery was that its bombers were exclusively for nuclear delivery. The problem with the strategy of "massive retaliation" was that the Communists responded with proxy wars and insurgencies for which the use of nuclear weapons would have been grossly disproportionate. The Kennedy administration brought a new national strategy of "flexible response," which provided for options on the full spectrum of warfare including counterinsurgency and conventional warfare.

In accordance with the strategy of "flexible response," some B-52Fs were modified to carry two Multiple Ejector Racks (MER) on the Hound Dog missile pylons under the South Bay and later Sun Bath projects. Each MER carried six bombs, increasing the load of the aircraft to 51 conventional bombs. Thirty B-52F bombers departed Andersen AFB, Guam, on 18 June 1965 to fly the first Arc Light strike against targets in Vietnam. In an inversion of their usual missions, the strategic B-52s were used against tactical targets in South Vietnam, while the tactical fighters (mostly F-105 Thunderchiefs and F-4 Phantom IIs) flew the strategic missions into North Vietnam.

Beginning in late 1965, the B-52D fleet received a comprehensive package of modifications for conventional bombing missions. In addition to the installation of MERs on the wing pylons, the aircraft were painted in camouflage and got the Big Belly improvement in the bomb bay to carry 84 Mk 82 or 42 M117 bombs internally. The first B-52Ds arrived at Andersen AFB in March 1966 and the last B-52F departed the war zone the next month.

Arc Light raids were partly successful. The challenge was to find elusive Communist targets and hit them before they moved. When this was done, the effect on troops, supplies, bunkers and tunnels was devastating. But often the only result was the widespread destruction of uninhabited jungle. The long flights from Andersen AFB to Vietnam also put much wear on the airplanes and required ample support from KC-135A tankers. The United States obtained basing rights for some B-52Ds at U-Tapao in Thailand, which was much closer to Vietnam. Missions from U-Tapao began in 1967.

While the B-52Ds fought the war in Vietnam, the older B-52B, C, E, and some F models were retired. The B-52G and H models stood alert with nuclear weapons to maintain a deterrent posture, which, regardless of Vietnam, remained SAC's primary mission. By 1972, the United States was drawing down its presence in Vietnam despite the stalled peace talks. So when North Vietnam launched a major offensive against the South in March 1972, the fastest response that the United States could make was with airpower. Under Operation Bullet Shot, the B-52 force at U-Tapao and Andersen AFB was massively reinforced, including the first introduction of B-52Gs into the war zone. Bombing of strategic targets in North Vietnam had been halted since 1968, but resumed in 1972 with Operation Linebacker. The first B-52 raid against North Vietnam took place on 9 April 1972, and the first B-52 was lost to North Vietnamese air defenses on 22 November 1972.

The North Vietnamese broke off peace negotiations on 13 December 1972. Frustrated by the impasse, President Richard M. Nixon authorized Operation Linebacker II. For the first time in the war, the B-52 force was unleashed to use its maximum conventional capability against targets in North Vietnam. During the so-called "Eleven Days of Christmas" between 18 December and 29 December 1972, B-52s supported by tactical jets caused heavy damage to targets in the Hanoi and Haiphong regions. The B-52s dropped 15,000 tons of bombs in 729 sorties, at the cost of nine B-52Ds and B-52Gs shot down and many others damaged. Of the 92 crewmembers on those aircraft, 26 were recovered, 33 killed or missing in action, and 33 captured by enemy forces.

Interestingly, the more modern B-52G proved to be less successful than the older B-52D during Linebacker II. The lighter structure of the B-52G was more vulnerable to catastrophic failure after suffering combat damage. The B-52D fleet had the Phase V electronic countermeasures suite, whereas most B-52Gs had the less effective Phase IV systems. The B-52G fleet also lacked the wing-mounted MERs or the Big Belly modifications, so they only carried 27 bombs.

From a political perspective, Linebacker II was an outstanding success, forcing North Vietnam back to peace negotiations that concluded with the signing of the Paris Peace Accords on 27 January 1973. B-52 strikes in Cambodia and Laos continued until 15 August 1973, when the last combat mission was flown.

B-52G 58-0244 approaches to land at Andersen AFB, Guam a few days before the first Operation Linebacker II attack on North Vietnam in December 1972. This aircraft had dark green (FS34079), blue green (FS34159) and tan (FS34201) on its upper surfaces and gloss white (FS17875) on its bottom. A B-52D waits beside the runway. (USAF)

Operation Desert Storm

After the Vietnam War, the B-52 Stratofortress force decreased in size. The B-52F fleet was fully retired in 1978 and the last B-52D left the force in 1983. These reductions left only the B-52G and B-52H in service with SAC, in addition to the one highly modified NB-52B assigned to NASA.

In response to the launch of Iraq's invasion of Kuwait on 2 August 1990, President George H. W. Bush ordered Operation Desert Shield to begin on 6 August 1990. The objective of Operation Desert Storm was to protect Saudi Arabia and its vital oil fields in the event that Iraqi forces continued to advance after conquering Kuwait.

Amongst the deployments in support of Operation Desert Shield were B-52Gs from several wings to Diego Garcia, a British territory that had been turned into an American base because its proximity to the Middle East and Southwest Asia. The deploying airplanes and personnel comprised the 4300th BW (Provisional). The first B-52G landed on Diego Garcia on 12 August. By 16 August, the 4300th BW (Provisional) had 20 B-52G aircraft ready to attack Iraqi forces if they invaded Saudi Arabia.

On 17 January 1991, the coalition led by the United States launched Operation Desert Storm, whose primary objective was to liberate Kuwait from Iraqi occupation. The supporting objectives were to destroy Iraqi military forces and supporting industrial capabilities, including programs to develop weapons of mass destruction. The first B-52G action of Operation Desert Storm was a missile attack by seven B-52Gs launched from Barksdale AFB against strategic targets in Iraq, in an attack described in more detail later in this book. Shortly after that action, the 4300th BW (Provisional) launched night low-level bombing missions against Iraqi airfields. Despite the predictions of 30% losses, the suppression of Iraqi air defenses was so effective that no B-52Gs were shot down. After the first attacks, some of the 4300th BW (Provisional) force landed at King 'Abd al-'Azîz International Airport, north of Jiddah on Saudi Arabia's west coast, to form the initial complement of the 1708th BW (Provisional). During the war, other B-52G sorties were generated from the 801st BW (Provisional), Morón AB, Spain, and the 806th BW (Provisional), RAF Fairford, United Kingdom.

After the first few days, B-52G attacks shifted to high-altitude area bombing, primarily of Iraqi ground forces, logistics facilities, and lines of communication. The attacks depleted and demoralized the enemy in preparation for the ground offensive. B-52Gs dropped 30% of total Coalition bomb tonnage in 1,624 sorties during Operation Desert Storm. Electrical system failure caused the loss of one B-52G (59-2593) and the death of three crewmen on 3 February 1991.

B-52G 59-2598 deployed from the 93rd BMW, Castle AFB to the 1708th BW (Provisional), King 'Abd al-'Azîz International Airport, near Jiddah, Saudi Arabia, for Operation Desert Storm. The wing pylons and presumably the bomb bay are loaded with M117 bombs as it departs on a combat mission. Most 1708th BW (Provisional) missions targeted Iraqi ground forces. (Senior Airman Chris Putnam / USAF)

Members of the 1708th Munitions Maintenance Squadron, 1708th BW (Provisional) load an M-117R 750-pound bombs onto a B-52G Stratofortress bomber aircraft during Operation Desert Storm. The M117R had a MAU-91/B retarding set for low altitude delivery, in contrast to the M117 with MAU-103/B low-drag conical fins on page 45, which was for high altitude delivery. (Senior Airman Chris Putnam / USAF)

The Cold War Ends

With the entry of the B-1B Lancer into operational service, B-52Gs began to be retired to the Aerospace Maintenance and Regeneration Center (AMARC) at Davis-Monthan Air Force Base (AFB) in Arizona in 1989. At AMARC, the aircraft were first picked over for parts and then scrapped. Scrapping a B-52 was an elaborate process that involved severing the wings from the fuselage, breaking up the fuselage into several pieces, and then arranging all the parts on the ground in a specified pattern. The purpose of this process was to present unambiguous evidence to Soviet reconnaissance satellites passing overhead that the B-52 was in fact scrapped and no longer could be counted against the limits of arms-control treaties.

By 1991, B-52s had served in two conventional wars, but the primary mission of the airplane remained strategic deterrence of the Soviet Union. The world was changing rapidly, however, and the Cold War was coming to an end. The Berlin Wall fell in 1989, and the Warsaw Pact was dissolved in 1991. On 27 September 1991, President George H.W. Bush ordered SAC to remove its bombers and Minuteman II missiles from alert. The next day, the nuclear weapons were unloaded from the SAC alert force of B-52 and B-1 bombers, which with the alert tanker fleet, were stood down. In December 1991, the Soviet Union crumbled. That the Cold War had ended on favorable terms for the United States and without a nuclear war was the ultimate sign that the B-52 had accomplished its mission. In the words of General George L. Butler, commander in chief of SAC (CINCSAC): ". . . rest secure in the knowledge that for the first time in over 40 years we can truly promise our children and our grandchildren a world drained from the tension of superpower confrontation. God bless you all for what you have accomplished. CINCSAC out."

The end of the Cold War left SAC without a primary mission. Also, analysis of the results of Operation Desert Storm led to a rethinking of the organization of the U.S. Air Force. During the Cold War, SAC had been tasked with the "strategic" mission of deterring – and, if necessary, fighting – a nuclear war against the Soviet Union, while the Tactical Air Command (TAC) had the responsibility for fighter and attack aircraft used to wage regional wars. What had actually happened during Operation Desert Storm was that most of the "strategic" attacks against targets in Iraq were conducted by TAC fighters, while the B-52G bombers of SAC were mostly employed in the "tactical" mission of attacking ground forces. Meanwhile, the SAC tankers were used for the benefit of all forces and not just SAC bombers. These trends had already been noticed during the Vietnam War but had not been acted on as long as the nuclear mission was paramount.

When the nuclear mission was relegated to secondary importance, the time was right to reorganize the U.S. Air Force. SAC's bombers and reconnaissance aircraft were merged

B-52H 61-0006 shows the fighter-style tail codes painted on bombers after the transition from SAC to Air Combat Command (ACC). The code LA is assigned to the 2nd BW, Barksdale AFB. The tail flash on this aircraft is yellow, signifying that it is assigned to the 11th BS and the 11th Aircraft Maintenance Unit of the 2nd BW. The ACC emblem in subdued colors is between the tail stripe and the LA tail code. (Author)

Aerospace Maintenance and Regeneration Center (AMARC) was the last stop for the B-52G fleet. Some parts were salvaged to use on the B-52H fleet. Wings were removed, and the fuselage was cut into three pieces. After the airframe was sliced up, the pieces were arranged for overhead observation to verify compliance with the Strategic Arms Reduction Treaty (START). (Jerry Fugere)

with the assets of TAC to form the new Air Combat Command (ACC) on 1 June 1992, while SAC tankers joined the airlifters of the Military Airlift Command to form the new Air Mobility Command (AMC).

The assignment of the B-52 wings to ACC affected the appearance of the aircraft: their tails were marked with the two-letter wing codes and the ACC emblem.

Another change that followed Operation Desert Storm was the removal of the gunners from the B-52 crews, effective 1 October 1991. Although the B-52H crew was reduced to five members, the gunner's ejection seat and crew station remained in place. In 1994, the guns began to be removed from the B-52Hs and were replaced by perforated plates.

A significant B-52 unit during this period of transition was the 34th BS. The 34th BS was assigned to the 366th Wing (WG) at Mountain Home AFB, Idaho, although it was based at Castle AFB, California, to benefit from the specialized B-52 maintenance capabilities of the 93rd BW at that base. The 366th WG was an ACC experiment to create a rapid intervention force. The former TAC practice of organizing its aircraft into "pure" wings of fighters or attack aircraft simplified peacetime logistics and training. In combat, commanders created ad hoc strike packages of multiple types of aircraft from different units. The 366th WG was an attempt to create a unit that would fight in wartime as it trained in peacetime. The 34th BS, with its complement of eight B-52Gs, was the first B-52 operational squadron to be assigned to a wing predominantly equipped with fighters. The assignment of the B-52G to the 34th BS was short-lived; it was replaced in 1994 by the B-1B. The 366th WG was a laboratory for the integration of bombers and fighters within ACC.

ACC had two B-52 mishaps. B-52H 61-0026, assigned to the 325th BS, 92nd BW, crashed on 24 June 1994. The mishap was caused by a reckless pilot who flew unsafe maneuvers during practice for an airshow. B-52H 60-052, a 20th BS, 2nd BW aircraft deployed at the time of its loss to the 20th Expeditionary Bomb Squadron, 36th WG, crashed in the Pacific Ocean, 30 miles northwest of Guam, on 21 July 2008.

During the Cold War, the Air Force Reserve had never been assigned the bomber mission, which required the ability to pull alert and launch combat missions within minutes of notification. With the end of the Cold War and the refocusing of the B-52 force away from strategic nuclear deterrence and toward conventional attack, the Air Force Reserve activated the 93rd BS, its first B-52 squadron, on 1 October 1993. The squadron was fully operational on 1 June 1995. Assigned to the 917th WG of the Air Force Reserve, the 93rd BS was collocated with the active-duty 2nd BW at Barksdale AFB to benefit from the existing investment in B-52 simulators and maintenance capability.

The on-going retirement of the B-52G fleet and the reassignment of the tankers from SAC to AMC also changed the disposition of the B-52 force. During the Cold War, SAC had organized the B-52 force into bombardment wings composed of one or two squadrons of B-52 bombers and one squadron of tankers, dispersed as widely as possible for protection against a Soviet surprise attack.

By 1995, all the B-52Gs had been retired, most B-52 wings had been deactivated, and the operational B-52H force was consolidated at Minot AFB, North Dakota, (23rd BS and the short-lived 72nd BS, 5th BW) and Barksdale AFB (11th BS, 20th BS, and 96th BS, 2nd BW; and 93rd BS, 917th WG).

These B-52Hs are parked on the "Christmas Tree" at Minot AFB Alert Parking Area in 2004. Although it is no longer routine for bombers to be loaded with nuclear weapons and placed on alert, the force can be placed back on alert status within 24 hours. (Author)

A crew chief directs the pilots of a B-52H Stratofortress onto the flightline during an exercise at Barksdale AFB on 1 February 2005. (Airman 1st Class Trina R. Flannagan / USAF)

From top, a B-52H, a B-1B, and a B-2A fly in formation. Each aircraft typified a different generation of aircraft design. Together they formed the core of U.S. Air Force global striking power. (USAF)

B-52 Aft Fuselage Modification

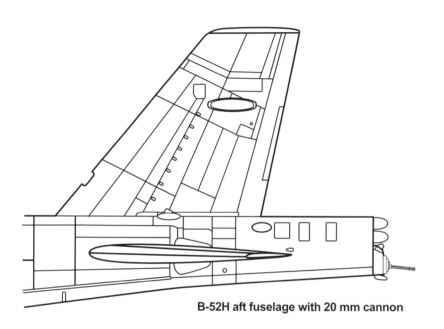

B-52H aft fuselage with 20 mm cannon

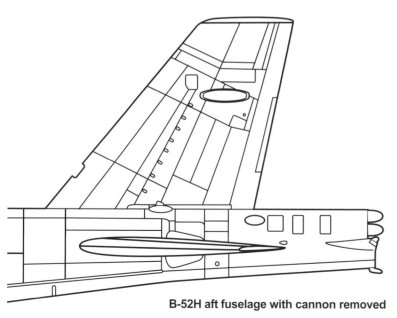

B-52H aft fuselage with cannon removed

The tail gun has been removed from this B-52H and replaced by a "cheese grater" plate. The radomes for the AN/ASG-21 defensive fire control system located above the "cheese grater" plate and the gunner crew station in the cockpit were not removed. Given the ineffectiveness of the gun against modern fighters, the costs of gunners and defensive gun maintenance could no longer be justified. (Author)

B-52H 61-0021 leads a formation from the 93rd BS. Aircraft with the 93rd BS were identified by the BD code, blue and gold checked tail flash, "AFRC" (Air Force Reserve Command) on the tail, and Indian head logo on the tip tanks. (USAF)

On 1-3 August 1994, this B-52H, 60-0059, flew around the world nonstop with 60-0008 to demonstrate the global striking power of ACC. The 2nd BW emblem in subdued colors was just aft of the nose art. (USAF)

The Benefield Anechoic Facility (BAF) at Edwards AFB, California, was the largest anechoic chamber in the world and the only one able to hold a B-52. BAF supported installed systems testing for avionics test programs requiring a large, shielded chamber with radio frequency absorption capability that simulated free space. (USAF)

An F-16B of the 412th Test Wing flies safety chase for a B-52H on a test mission. Safety chase aircraft were typically used when bombs or missiles were being dropped in flight test. Flight testing has always been an essential component of B-52 modernization. (USAF)

A B-17G Flying Fortress and a B-52H Stratofortress fly in a Heritage Flight formation in 2006. Only 18 years separate the delivery of these two particular aircraft, so it is possible that the same individuals may have flown or maintained both aircraft. With the B-52H still in service after 50 years, the current generation of airmen may be using the same aircraft as their grandfathers. With a planned B-52H retirement date of 2040, the last B-52 personnel have not yet been born. (Master Sgt. Michael A. Kaplan / USAF)

B-52H 60-0033 *Instrument of Destruction* was with the 23rd BS, 5th BW, at Minot AFB in 2004. (Author)

B-52H 60-0047 *North Dakota Payback* was with the 23rd BS, 5th BW, at Minot AFB, North Dakota, in 2004. (Author)

B-52H 60-0018 *POW MIA You Are Not Forgotten* was with the 23rd BS, 5th BW, at Minot AFB in 2004. (Author)

B-52H 60-0044 *Excalibur* was with the 23rd BS, 5th BW, at Minot AFB in 2004. Lieutenant Colonel Robert P. Bender, Jr. was the commander of the 5th Operations Support Squadron. (Author)

B-52H 60-0055 *War Eagle* was with the 23rd BS, 5th BW, at Minot AFB in 2004. It was marked as the flagship of the 5th Operations Group, commanded by Colonel Eric N. Single. The previous nose art had clearly been painted over with fresh paint that contrasted with the base coat. (Author)

B-52H 60-0052 *Hot Stuff* was with the 96th BS, 2nd BW, at Barksdale AFB in 2004. Later reassigned to the 20th BS, 2th BW, it crashed on 21 July 2008 off the coast of Guam, killing all six crewmembers. (Technical Sgt. Robert J. Horstman / USAF)

B-52H 60-0001 *Memphis Belle IV* was the first B-52H. Assigned to the 20th BS, 2nd BW in 2004, it maintained the *Memphis Belle* tradition. (Author)

Memphis Belle IV was the only B-52 to have nose art on both sides. The belle was wearing a blue swimsuit on the left and red on the right. (Author)

B-52H 60-0028 *Tired Eagle* was with the 96th BS, 2nd BW, at Barksdale AFB in 2004. (Author)

Tired Eagle was marked as the flagship of the historic 8th Air Force, parent organization to both the 2nd BW and 5th BW. (Author)

B-52H 60-0035 *Global Warrior* was with the 11th BS, 2nd BW, at Barksdale AFB in 2005. Unlike during World War II, nose art is strictly reviewed and subject to command approval. (Author)

B-52H 60-0036 *Tagboard Flyer* was with the 6519th Flight Test Squadron, 412th Test Wing, at Edwards AFB in 2004. Earlier, this aircraft had been a mothership for the Lockheed D-21B Tagboard reconnaissance drone. (Author)

B-52H 60-0061 *Command Decision* was with the 11th BS, 2nd BW, at Barksdale AFB in 2005. (Author)

B-52H 61-0029 *SAC Time* was with the 93rd BS, 917th WG, at Barksdale AFB in 2005. (Author)

Offensive Avionics

The AN/ASQ-176 OAS became operational in 1982 and proved to be highly successful in service – reliable, accurate, and enabling the addition of the ALCM to the B-52 arsenal. The Block II software for the OAS, which entered service several years after OAS did, added the Common Strategic Rotary Launcher (CSRL) and Advanced Cruise Missile (ACM) to improve the nuclear strike capability of the B-52. The only conventional weapons that could be delivered by OAS were gravity bombs and cluster bombs.

Even before the end of the Cold War, SAC had a requirement to use the B-52Gs that were not equipped for ALCM as conventional bombers. One obstacle to implementing this capability was the architecture of the OAS software, which tightly integrated all the functions of the system. As a result, changing anything in the software (for example, adding a new type of weapon) required the complete retesting of every OAS function in the laboratory and in flight. With an array of precision-guided munitions in the development pipeline, the amount of regression testing was predicted to be unaffordable. Therefore, the Air Force and Boeing redesigned the architecture of the OAS software. The navigation function of OAS would not change often, so the associated software from OAS Block II was repackaged as the Flight Management System (FMS). Each

type of weapon would have its own associated module of OAS software called a Stores Management Overlay (SMO).

With the FMS/SMO modular architecture, the addition of a new weapon to the inventory would require only the development and testing of the new SMO, and not the FMS or the other SMOs. Although invisible from the outside of the aircraft, the new FMS/SMO architecture of the OAS software was a critical enabler for the future of the B-52.

Another important change to the OAS was the addition of Global Positioning System (GPS) satellite navigation. GPS had not been operational when OAS entered service, and SAC was reluctant to use a navigation system that was external to the aircraft and might not survive a nuclear attack. The entry of GPS into operational service in the 1990s, the new emphasis on conventional warfare for the B-52, and the greater precision required for conventional weapons all combined to drive the integration of GPS into the OAS. The most visible sign of the addition of GPS was the new GPS antenna on the top of the fuselage between the wings and the KY-920/A data entry keyboard for the GPS installed at the navigator's crew station.

The offensive sensors of the B-52 also were replaced. In the late 1980s, the AN/APQ-

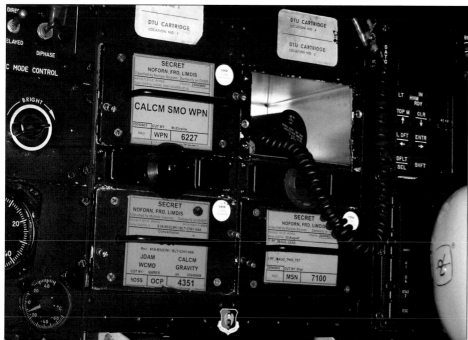

Three of the four bays of this Data Transfer Unit (DTU) are filled by Data Transfer Unit Cartridges (DTUC). A DTUC contains magnetic tape. The DTUCs are loaded with the Flight Management System (FMS), the Stores Management Overlays (SMO) for conventional weapons, and the mission data. The DTUCs are marked with the security classification of the data that they contain. (Author)

The navigator sits downstairs in a windowless compartment facing the OAS panel. The radar navigator sits to the left of the navigator, facing a similar panel. The navigator has two main displays. Above the displays is the DTU. The navigator's right hand is on the Integrated Keyboard (IKB), which also has a trackball. To the left of the navigator's left hand is the keyboard for the Global Positioning System (GPS). (Author)

27

166 Strategic Radar replaced the original OAS radar in the B-52H. By the 1990s, the AN/ASQ-151 EVS was aging rapidly and was no longer supportable. The Hughes AN/AAQ-6 Forward Looking Infrared (FLIR) was replaced by the Loral (now Lockheed Martin) AN/AAQ-23 FLIR. The Westinghouse AN/AVQ-22 Steerable Television System (STV) was replaced by the BAE Systems AN/AVQ-37. The new EVS sensors were more reliable, easier to maintain, and had better availability of spare parts.

As OAS approached 20 years in operational service, it faced the same problem as EVS, with the imminent unavailability of spare parts for certain subsystems. In response, the Air Force launched the Avionics Midlife Improvement (AMI) program. AMI was primarily a reliability, maintainability, and supportability modification that replaced certain parts of the OAS. It preserved B-52 combat capability and upgraded avionics systems based on 1970s technology that had support and capability problems. AMI replaced the Avionics Computer Unit and Data Transfer Unit of the OAS, both of which had severe limitations, and replaced the INS, for which manufacturer support was ending. The project also rehosted the OAS software in the Ada 95 language. The AMI program began development in the year 2000, with flight tests beginning in 2003. The first combat-ready B-52H with AMI became operational in 2006.

After AMI, the next step in B-52H offensive avionics modernization was the Combat Network Communication Technology (CONECT) project. The most visible change

The GPS-controlled reception pattern antenna is located on top of the B-52H fuselage, near where the leading edge of the wings joins the fuselage. The antenna is unpainted. The dome ahead of the GPS antenna is for the AN/ASC-19 AFSATCOM satellite communications system. The dome aft of the GPS antenna is for the Miniature Receive Terminal. (Author)

The KY-920/A is part of the GPS system that was added to the B-52H, as was the IU power panel above it. The IU power panel is used to control the power to the GPS, load the key so the GPS receiver can use the encrypted GPS signal, and zeroize the key. (Author)

The sensor turret and fairing on the left side of the B-52H under the nose are for the Steerable Television System (STV) and the right sensor turret and fairing are for the Forward Looking Infrared (FLIR). The turrets can be turned to hide the windows for the EVS sensors to protect them against dirt and damage. (Author)

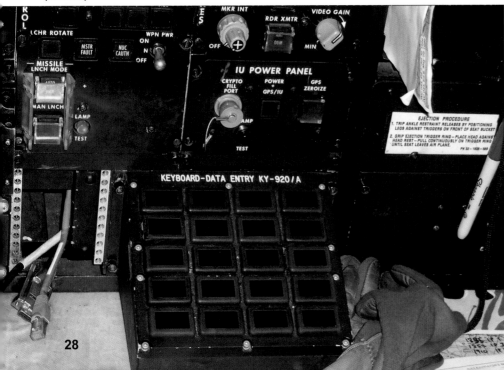

A test B-52H assigned to the 419th Flight Test Squadron has a CONECT color flat panel display installed at the radar navigator's right multifunction display position, but retains the legacy OAS monochrome display in the left position. The CONECT unit is able to display more information at a higher resolution than the legacy OAS monochrome display. (USAF)

Most AMI changes are not evident to the casual observer. The most obvious change is the new Data Transfer System above the navigator's left OAS display. With the new system, solid-state memory replaces magnetic tape. This B-52H has a CONECT color flat panel display in the navigator's right display position. (USAF)

In the 1980's the B-52H fleet was modernized with the AN/APQ-166 Strategic Radar. After nearly three decades in service, the AN/APQ-166 experienced systemic sustainment and parts obsolescence issues. It will be replaced with a new radar. The entire radome pivots up to allow access to the radar and other systems for maintenance. (Senior Airman Brian Ferguson / USAF)

This Litening AT targeting pod is suspended from the small pylon on the right wing of the B-52 between the two engine pods. Prominent external features of the pod are the steerable ball containing the FLIR head, television camera, and laser; a door to facilitate access to the interior of the pod for maintenance; and an intake for cooling air for the environmental control unit on the aft end of the pod. The Litening AT is 87 inches long, 16 inches in diameter, and weighs 440 pounds. The Litening AT is externally indistinguishable from the earlier Litening II and Litening ER. The Litening AT/ISR can be identified by a small radio antenna. (Author)

resulting from CONECT was the replacement of the antiquated monochrome avionics displays at the crew stations with color flat-panel displays. Less visible but equally important were the additions of a client/server architecture, a high-bandwidth data network, a Link-16 tactical data link, an advanced wideband terminal, and a new intercom system. The new architecture enabled the B-52H to receive in-flight target coordinates from an external source and download those coordinates to a guided weapon with no voice communications or manual data entry required by the B-52 crew. The target's coordinates were then displayed on full-color moving maps along with the aircraft's location and threat information. The result was a much faster cycle from detecting the target until its destruction. This feature is important when providing close air support to ground forces or attacking mobile time-sensitive targets such as mobile missile launchers. Boeing and the 419th Flight Test Squadron tested CONECT in flight during 2009-2011.

Litening Targeting Pod

The targeting pod selected for the B-52H was the Northrop Grumman AN/AAQ-28(V)1 Litening II. The Litening II was derived from the Litening I pod that was developed by the Israeli firm Rafael Armament Development Authority. Litening II contained a 256 x 256 pixel FLIR sensor, which displayed an infrared image of the target to the aircrew, and a television camera for visible light images. It was equipped with a laser designator for laser-guided munitions and a laser spot tracker/rangefinder. The targeting pod included an automatic target tracker. The pod gave B-52H crews the capability to acquire and positively identify targets without being dependent on an external observer and designate targets for laser-guided bombs.

On the B-52H, the Litening II was mounted beneath the right wing between the

The radar navigator uses his right hand to manipulate the Advanced Guided Weapon Control Panel (AGWCP) hand controller. The hand controller is used for pointing the steerable head of the targeting pod. (Author)

The AGWCP video monitor is installed above the radar navigator's left MFD. The video monitor displays television and FLIR imagery. The AGWCP is to the left of the video monitor and left MFD. (Author)

inboard and outboard engine pods. It required a special display and control panel called the Advanced Guided Weapon Control Panel (AGWCP) at the radar navigator crew station. Only a few B-52H aircraft were wired for Litening II.

The 93rd BS, 917th WG, was given the responsibility for testing and operating the Litening II on the B-52H, with Lt. Col. Keith "Hands" Schultz and Maj. Paul "Charcoal" Harper as project pilots and Lt. Col. William "Sleepy" Floyd as project radar navigator. In January 2003, the test team brought 61-0008 and 61-0021 to the Utah Test and Training Range to put Litening II though its paces. By March 2003, the testing was completed and the B-52H with Litening II headed off to war.

Northrop Grumman improved Litening. The first upgrade was the AN/AAQ-28(V)6 Litening ER, which featured a 640 x 512 pixel FLIR that had higher resolution and 25 percent longer range. The AN/AAQ-28A(V)1 Litening AT added image enhancement and the ability to generate target coordinates for GPS-guided weapons. It became operational on the B-52H with 93rd BS, 917th WG, in 2006. The AN/AAQ-28A(V)3 Litening AT/ISR (Intelligence, Surveillance, and Reconnaissance) added a radio link to transmit imagery from the pod to a ground station, which improved coordination when conducting close air support missions.

Sniper Targeting Pod

An alternative to the Litening pod was the Lockheed Martin AN/AAQ-33 Sniper targeting pod. Previously used on the A-10C, B-1B, F-16C/D, F-15E, CF-188 (Canadian F/A-18A/B), Harrier GR.7/GR.9 and Tornado aircraft, the Sniper pod was later integrated with the B-52H. Sniper pod integration on the B-52 provided aircrews with laser target designation, positive target identification, target geo-location, and video downlink capability to ground forces.

A Sniper pod contained a high-definition forward looking infrared (FLIR), laser rangefinder and designator, laser spot tracker, laser marker, high-definition television camera, video data link, and digital data recorder. All of this equipment was packed in a pod only 98.2 inches long, 11.9 inches in diameter and weighing 446 pounds.

In a typical combat situation, a Sniper-equipped B-52H would be working with a ground-based Joint Terminal Attack Controller (JTAC) attached to a U.S. Army, U.S. Marine Corps or allied infantry unit. Using his GPS and laser rangefinder, the JTAC could locate the enemy very accurately. Entering coordinates provided by the JTAC into OAS, the B-52H crew would fly towards the unit in need of close air support. The Sniper pod would point its sensors at the location requested by the JTAC and, using its video data link, provide the JTAC with a view from above. Depending in the lighting and atmospheric conditions, the sensor of choice might be the FLIR or the high-definition television camera. With the B-52H radar navigator and JTAC looking at the same imagery, the chances of hitting the wrong target would be greatly reduced. If the target moved (for example, an automobile in motion), the Sniper pod would automatically track it. After the JTAC cleared the B-52H to attack the target, the Sniper pod typically would designate the target for a laser-guided bomb.

Another scenario would be an intelligence, surveillance and reconnaissance mission, where the B-52H crew searched for targets using the FLIR or high-definition television

The AN/AAQ-33 Sniper targeting pod was mounted on the same pylon used by the AN/AAQ-28 Litening targeting pod. (Staff Sgt. Michael Andriacco / USAF)

The upper left monitor at the radar navigator's crew station was for Litening or Sniper imagery. It was a replacement for the AGWCP. (Staff Sgt. Christopher Boitz / USAF)

The keyboard above the navigator's right Multi-Function Display (MFD) is for the demand assigned multiple access (DAMA) modem associated with the AN/ARC-210(V). The keyboard to the right of the DAMA keyboard is for the AN/ASC-19 AFSATCOM system. Satellite communications enables greater tactical flexibility and were heavily used in combat operations. (Author)

The AN/ARC-210(V) radio control panel is located on the overhead panel between the pilot and co-pilot. The AN/ARC-210(V) gives the B-52H crew the capability to communicate with all the participants on a battlefield with encrypted and anti-jam communications. To the left of the panel is the toggle switch for night vision goggle-compatible lighting in the cockpit. (Author)

camera. Identifying a target, the Sniper pod could use its laser rangefinder and the navigation information from the OAS to calculate the coordinates of the target, to be passed on to others or used for delivery of its own weapons. The B-52H could use the laser marker in the Sniper pod to point out the target to troops on the ground or aircrew in other aircraft, the infrared marker beam being invisible to the naked eye but visible to a person wearing night vision goggles.

The Litening and Sniper pods radically transformed the role of the B-52. Originally designed to execute missions independently against known fixed targets, the B-52H with the latest navigation, communications and targeting avionics had the capability to work closely with other aircraft and ground units to find and attack mobile, fleeting targets in a networked environment.

Communications Upgrades

SAC had marvelous global communications for its era, with the requirement of surviving a first strike by the Soviet Union and then ordering retaliation. The shift from a nuclear to a conventional emphasis required the B-52H to have enhanced communications systems. Whereas nuclear attacks would have been highly scripted affairs that required no communications after the order was given to execute, conventional missions might require a B-52H to launch with no particular target, fly to a combat zone, and only then receive specific targets from a Combined Air Operations Center (CAOC) or a Forward Air Controller (FAC) in a fighter or on the ground. This meant that the B-52H needed communication systems with higher bandwidth and a greater range of frequencies and modes.

The AN/ARC-210(V) Very High Frequency/Ultra High Frequency (VHF/UHF) radio system was added to the B-52H. It provided air-to-air and air-to-ground communication in both line of sight (LOS) and satellite communication (SATCOM) modes. The set used a tuneable LOS antenna, a SATCOM antenna, a control panel, and a receiver-transmitter.

The VHF/UHF radio transceiver had selectable commercial Have Quick I and Have Quick II anti-jamming, single-channel ground-air radio system (SINCGARS) modes; demand assigned multiple access (DAMA) operation; and manual maritime modes. It was also capable of data transmission with a data rate up to 32,000 bits per second. The frequency range of the AN/ARC-210(V) radio was 30 to 399.9875 MHz, tunable at 5 kHz intervals. Channel spacing was 25 kHz in all bands.

The AN/ARR-85(V) Miniature Receive Terminal (MRT) was also installed on the B-52H fleet starting in the mid-1990s. The MRT provided a Very Low Frequency/Low Frequency (VLF/LF) receive-only capability for the aircraft. The MRT was controlled by the navigator and was designed to automatically receive, process, and print messages at extended ranges in nuclear and jamming environments over the frequency band of 14 to 60 KHz. The MRT consisted of a receiver, transfer module, remote control unit (RCU), automatic data processing printer, and an antenna subsystem that contained two transverse electric (TE) antennas and one transverse magnetic (TM) antenna. Messages were received through the antennas and processed in the MRT receiver, and intelligent data was output to the printer. The MRT provided a highly survivable means of notifying the B-52H crew through the MILSTAR satellites of Emergency Action Messages (EAM). In the event a B-52H was launched on a nuclear strike mission, the aircrew would require an authorization via EAM to proceed past its positive-control turnaround point and deliver the nuclear weapons.

In the 1990s, computer and communications technology for consumer and commercial applications developed so rapidly that the military acquisition system could not keep up with it. In order to provide B-52H crews with the networking and situational awareness benefits of the latest technology, the Air Force developed the Falcon View and later the Combat Track II systems, which put laptop computers in the B-52H with specialized moving map software linked to satellite navigation and communications. The B-52H had three computers, one each at the pilot, radar navigator/navigator, and electronic warfare officer crew stations. These systems proved to be highly useful in combat.

B-52H 60-0029 of the 69th BS, 5th BW takes off from Andersen AFB with a full load of M117 bombs and a Litening targeting pod on the right wing between the inboard and outboard pairs of engines. (Senior Airman Carlin Leslie / USAF)

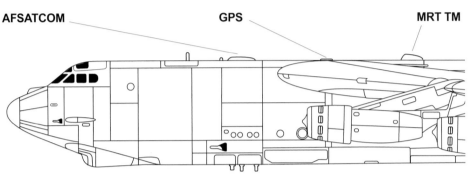

Antenna Installation

AFSATCOM   GPS   MRT TM

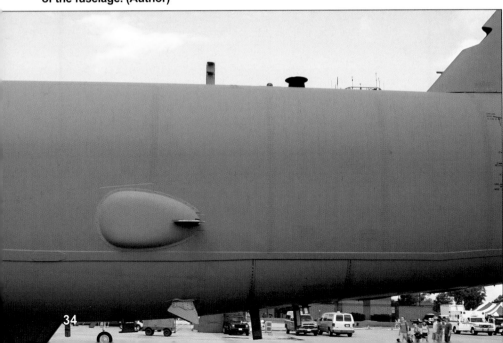

The transverse magnetic (TM) antenna for the AN/ARR-85 Miniature Receive Terminal (MRT) is located in the dome aft of the GPS antenna on the top of the fuselage and between the wings. (Author)

The circular antenna located between the ECM antenna and the vertical tail is for AN/ARC-210(V) satellite communications. The dome on the side of the fuselage is a transverse electric (TE) antenna for the MRT, with another TE antenna on the other side of the fuselage. (Author)

The Combat Track II display for the pilots folds up when they need full visibility out the windshield. Combat Track II displays are also used by the electronic warfare officer and the navigators. Combat Track II gives the B-52H crew an interim capability to operate as part of the network-centric battlefield and use space-based information sources, pending the fielding of the future Combat Network Communication Technology (CONECT) upgrade. (Author)

34

Nuclear Weapons

Nuclear Bombs

During the Cold War, the primary mission of the B-52 was to deliver nuclear bombs at intercontinental ranges. The service entry of the Mark 28, Mark 41, and Mark 53 thermonuclear weapons roughly coincided with the service entry of the B-52G and B-52H. The Mark 28 was produced in larger quantities than any other American nuclear bomb. It was much smaller than its predecessors and the B-52 could carry up to eight B28 bombs internally, increasing the number of targets able to be destroyed by a sortie. At 25 megatons, the Mark 41 was the largest yield nuclear weapon ever built by the United States. In practice, it was overkill for any actual targets. Less powerful but still with a staggering yield of nine megatons, the Mark 53 was a specialized weapon targeted against deeply buried Soviet command bunkers. Two Mark 41 or Mark 53 bombs filled the B-52 bomb bay. In 1968, the Mark 28, Mark 41 and Mark 53 weapons were redesignated as B28, B41, and B53 respectively.

The next generation of light-weight nuclear bombs emphasized improved safety and security features, and improved capability for high-speed low-altitude delivery. The B61 first supplemented and then gradually replaced the B28. The B83 had a one-megaton yield and was the last all-new American nuclear bomb, entering service in 1983.

After the end of the Cold War, the B-52H remained armed with the B61, the B83

The B83 was streamlined for high-speed low-altitude delivery. The aft section of the bomb contained a parachute, which allowed the bomb to descend to the ground for a surface burst without breaking up, and also gave the delivery aircraft time to escape the fireball. This item is a BDU-46/E, a dummy B83 used for training load crews. (Master Sgt. Ken Hammond / USAF)

Fuzed for surface detonation, the 9 megaton B53 would have dug a massive crater and crushed underground targets with a powerful shockwave. (National Nuclear Security Administration)

A munitions load crew muscles an MHU-7/M trailer containing a MHU-14/C clip-in rack holding four B28 bombs into the bay of a B-52H. (Technical Sgt. Boyd Belcher / USAF)

B-52D 56-0695 launches a GAM-72 (ADM-20) Quail decoy. Four Quails were carried on a carriage, which lowered the decoy for wing extension and engine start before launch. (USAF)

and a handful of B53 bombs, the latter being retired when the B61-11 penetrating bomb entered service on the B-2A bomber.

Quail

When the B-52 entered service, its high speed and altitude combined with electronic countermeasures and night/all-weather capabilities were sufficient to provide a high probability of successfully penetrating the rudimentary Soviet air defense. As the Soviet Union upgraded its air defense with improved radars, jet interceptors, and the first generation of surface-air missiles, SAC became interested in equipping its bombers with air-ground missiles and air-launched decoys that would enable it to strike targets outside the range of enemy air defenses. The McDonnell GAM-72 Quail was a decoy powered by a General Electric J85-GE-7 engine. It was designed to replicate the flight characteristics and radar signature of a B-52. Four Quails could be carried in half of the bomb bay. The Quail flew a programmed flight path, drawing fire away from the B-52. Quail entered SAC service in 1960, was redesignated ADM-20 in 1963 and was retired in 1978.

Hound Dog

The North American GAM-77 Hound Dog carried a W-28 thermonuclear warhead to destroy heavily defended targets. One missile was carried under each wing, between the inboard engine pod and the fuselage. The Hound Dog's Pratt & Whitney J52-P-3 turbojet engine propelled it to supersonic speeds after launch. The Hound Dog entered SAC service on the B-52G in 1961. Hound Dog and Quail were also retrofitted to earlier models of the B-52 and used on the B-52H after the cancellation of the Skybolt missile. After the introduction of the missiles, the typical weapons load for a B-52

B-52H 60-0006 carries GAM-77 (AGM-28) Hound Dog missiles. The Hound Dog was the first air-launched nuclear missile used by SAC. (John W. Ramsay Research Library, New England Air Museum collection)

B-52H 60-0022 carries four GAM-87 (AGM-48) Skybolt missiles. The Skybolt was cancelled during development and never saw production or operation service. (John W. Ramsay Research Library, New England Air Museum collection)

standing nuclear alert was two external Hound Dogs, and four Quails and one to four thermonuclear bombs in the bomb bay. Hound Dog was redesignated AGM-28 in 1963. The Hound Dog was never well regarded in service. The missile and its pylon had high drag, reducing the range of the B-52. The missile was unreliable and inaccurate. Hound Dog left operational service in 1976.

Skybolt

The Douglas GAM-87 Skybolt was the intended primary armament of the B-52H. Armed with a W-59 thermonuclear warhead and propelled by a two-stage Aerojet General solid rocket engine, the Skybolt was a ballistic missile completely invulnerable to contemporary air defenses. The Skybolt had a string of early flight test failures, and the program was cancelled in December 1962 although it was starting to show promise. Had it gone into service, the Skybolt also would have been used by Royal Air Force bombers. Although the program had already been cancelled, the Skybolt was redesignated the AGM-48A in 1963.

SRAM

The Boeing AGM-69A Short Range Attack Missile (SRAM) succeeded the problematic Hound Dog and the aborted Skybolt. Only fitted to the B-52G and B-52H, the SRAM was successful and had a long service life.

SRAM was propelled by a Lockheed SR75-LP-1 solid rocket motor to Mach 3 speeds,

Compared to the Hound Dog, the SRAM was smaller, faster and had a lower radar cross-section. (Master Sgt. Ken Hammond / USAF)

Early its life, the SRAM could also be carried on underwing pylons, six per pylon. External carriage of the SRAM only lasted for a few years. (USAF)

A SRAM Rotary Launcher loaded with eight missiles shares the bomb bay of a B-52H with four B28 bombs. (Technical Sgt. Boyd Belcher / USAF)

37

The SUU-67/A cruise missile pylon is a massive structure that can carry six Air Launched Cruise Missiles (ALCM). During Operation Desert Storm, the Conventional Air Launched Cruise Missile (CALCM) was launched from the B-52G and SUU-67/A. All subsequent combat launches of the CALCM have been from the B-52H and Common Strategic Rotary Launcher (CSRL). This SUU-67/A is carrying one ALCM. (Author)

A B-52G carries an AGM-109 during the ALCM fly-off. With its circular cross-section, the AGM-109 was easily distinguishable from the AGM-86B. The AGM-109 used the F107-WR-102 engine, the same engine as the AGM-86B, except repackaged to fit in the AGM-109 airframe. In the end, the U.S. Air Force chose the AGM-86B instead of the AGM-109. (USAF)

had inertial navigation and carried a W69 nuclear warhead. The B-52 carried SRAM on underwing pylons (six missiles on each pylon) and inside the bomb bay on a rotary launcher with eight missiles. The FB-111A also carried the SRAM. SRAM entered service in 1972.

With its high speed and low radar cross section, the SRAM was almost impossible to intercept. Although not highly accurate, it was accurate enough for its intended targets. With a typical nuclear alert load-out of four nuclear bombs and eight SRAMs in the bomb bay, SAC tactical doctrine was to use the SRAMs to destroy Soviet air-defense radar and surface-to-air missile sites, clearing the path for the B-52 to drop the bombs on military or industrial targets.

The SRAM was retired in 1990 due to the aging of its warhead and motor. The AGM-69B SRAM had been planned for the B-1A, but was cancelled with it. The AGM-131A SRAM II program faded away with the end of the Cold War.

Cruise Missiles

The cruise missile was the weapon that saved the B-52 from obsolescence. By the 1970s, the ability of the B-52 to penetrate the integrated air defenses of the Soviet Union was questionable. At the time, Boeing was developing a small drone called the Subsonic Cruise Aircraft Decoy (SCAD) to replace the obsolete ADM-20 Quail. The SCAD was intended to saturate air defenses and therefore increase the survivability of the B-52. The SCAD concept did not proceed, but with the addition of an accurate navigation system and a nuclear weapon, the SCAD become the AGM-86A Air Launched Cruise Missiles (ALCM), which could be carried in the B-52 bomb bay on the SRAM rotary launcher. The AGM-86A first flew in 1976. It never went into production but demonstrated the feasibility of the concept of a cruise missile that could be launched from the B-52 outside the range of enemy air defenses.

Boeing stretched the AGM-86A airframe to carry more fuel, with the extended missile being designated the AGM-86B. The U.S. Air Force conducted an ALCM fly-off between the Boeing AGM-86B and the General Dynamics-Convair AGM-109, which was a derivative of the Navy's Tomahawk sea-launched cruise missile. The first flight of an AGM-86B occurred in August 1979. In March 1980, the AGM-86B was declared winner of the fly-off. The AGM-86B entered service with the B-52Gs of the 668th BMS, 416th BMW, at Griffiss AFB, New York, in 1982. Production of the AGM-86B was completed in 1986.

The AGM-86B was eventually carried by some B-52Gs and all B-52Hs. The airplane needed the OAS to employ ALCM. Originally the ALCM was only carried on SUU-67/A pylons, with one SUU-67/A under each wing and each pylon carrying six missiles. Beside 12 AGM-86B missiles, the cruise-missile-modified B-52s continued to carry AGM-69A SRAM and nuclear bombs in the bomb bay. The ALCM enormously complicated the task of Soviet air defenses. In the event of a nuclear war, the Soviets would have had to intercept many ALCMs instead of a few bombers. Non-ALCM B-52Gs were primarily tasked with conventional missions.

After takeoff, the ALCM delivery sequence began when the navigator commanded the OAS to apply power to the ALCM and load its mission data. After the missile powered up, the transfer alignment sequence for the inertial navigation system (INS) of the ALCM began. The transfer alignment involved matching the attitude and velocities of the ALCM INS to those of the OAS. ALCM navigation accuracy was critically dependent on this transfer alignment, which required the radar navigator to accurately update the OAS with radar position fixes. The transfer alignment was tightened by the use of a transfer alignment (TAL) maneuver. During a TAL, the pilots turned tightly in one direction, then flew straight and level for a short period, then returned to the original heading with a tight turn. Before launch, the pilot had to toggle a consent switch at his crew station to prearm the W80-1 nuclear warhead of the ALCM. As the B-52 approached the cruise missile launch point, the OAS calculated when the missile was safe and in range (SAIR), which meant that the ALCM had sufficient range to reach the target. Once SAIR, the missile could be launched automatically by OAS or manually by the navigator using the launch button on the OAS weapon control panel. The AGM-86B was separated from the SUU-67/A by a MAU-12D/A ejector rack, which used a pyrotechnical cartridge to move a piston that pushed the ALCM away. As the ALCM separated from the MAU-12D/A, a lanyard pulled the engine inlet from its stowed position. The ALCM avionics first commanded pyrotechnics to fire so that the stabilizers and wings sprang into position, and then initiated the start sequence for the Williams International F107-WR-101 turbofan engine.

B-52G 58-0204 of the ALCM Combined Test Force, 6510th Test Wing carries a full load of 12 AGM-109 missiles during testing in 1979. (USAF)

This engine was a marvel of efficiency and miniaturization, and a critical enabling technology for the ALCM. With it, the ALCM had a range of approximately 1,500 miles. Under the guidance of the INS, the ALCM then flew several hours toward the target, navigating from waypoint to waypoint according to its mission data. By use of a radar altimeter, the ALCM could fly at low level to avoid detection. Over time, the INS position estimate would drift, degrading the accuracy of the ALCM flight path. To correct this drift, the AGM-86B used an ingenious technique called terrain contour matching (TERCOM).

Using terrain elevation maps of the Soviet Union based on data collected by reconnaissance satellites, mission planners created TERCOM maps over areas with distinctive topography. The mission data downloaded to the ALCM included these TERCOM maps. As the ALCM flew over terrain recorded on a TERCOM map, it used its INS, barometric altimeter, and radar altimeter to measure the elevation profile under its flight path. The ALCM computer compared the measured terrain elevation profile to the TERCOM map, precisely locating the actual location of the ALCM and providing a position update to the INS. TERCOM was dependent on a highly accurate transfer alignment before launch, because if the alignment were poor, the INS would drift so far that the ALCM would entirely miss the TERCOM map. A typical mission data load included several TERCOM maps of increasing resolution as the planned trajectory closed with the target. When the ALCM passed its penultimate waypoint, the W80-1 warhead was armed. The ALCM did not have countermeasures or make evasive maneuvers, but its low altitude and small size made it a difficult target. The navigation accuracy yielded a CEP of several tens of meters at the target, over which the W80-1 would be detonated at the selectable yield that had been programmed in the mission data. The combination

An AGM-109 rests on the ground at Dugway Proving Ground after a test mission. Test missiles deployed a parachute at the end of their missions. (USAF)

of high accuracy and thermonuclear effects would have resulted in a high probability of destroying all but the most hardened targets.

The AGM-86B revolutionized the nuclear striking power of the B-52 fleet in the last decade of the Cold War, but the U.S. Air Force continued to enhance this capability. The first improvement to ALCM capability was the A/A48K-1 CSRL. The CSRL was installed in the bomb bay of the B-52H only. Similar in concept to the SRAM rotary launcher, the CSRL was longer so it could carry the AGM-86B. To carry the CSRL, the B-52H required modification. With the addition of the CSRL carrying eight AGM-86B missiles, a full ALCM load for the B-52H increased to 20 missiles.

The AGM-86C CALCM was a highly classified variant of the AGM-86B developed under the Senior Surprise program. In the AGM-86C, a conventional blast/fragmentation warhead replaced the W80-1 and also displaced some fuel, giving the CALCM less range than the AGM-86B. The CALCM also added a GPS receiver, making it the first operational weapon guided by GPS. The CALCM first flew in August 1987 and was operational in 1988.

The combat debut for the CALCM was Operation Desert Storm, when seven B-52Gs of the 596th BMS, 2nd BMW, departed Barksdale AFB on 16 January 1991. The lead aircraft had the call sign "Doom 31" and was commanded by Lt. Col. Jay Beard, commander of the 596th BMS. "Doom 32" through "Doom 37" followed, with each bomber carrying CALCMs. As the force flew toward Iraq, the crews of their tankers noticed that the bombers were laden with cruise missiles.

Since only the nuclear-armed AGM-86B had been revealed and the tanker crews were not aware of the existence of the CALCM, the shocked tanker crews became convinced that the United States was going to initiate Operation Desert Storm with a nuclear attack. Nearly 15 hours after takeoff, the CALCMs were launched over Saudi Arabia at targets in Iraq and the B-52Gs turned for home. Of the 39 missiles carried, only 35 were launched because four were indicating problems. When the B-52Gs landed, they had each logged more than 35 hours of flight, making this the longest air combat mission in history to date. A year later, the CALCM was finally declassified and its combat debut was revealed.

Operation Desert Storm nearly exhausted the small stock of CALCMs, and Boeing converted more AGB-86Bs to the AGM-86C configuration. These early missiles were retroactively designated the CALCM Block 0. The next version was the CALCM Block 1, which featured avionics improvements, including a second-generation GPS receiver and software that doubled the navigational accuracy of the Block 0 CALCM. Block 1 also incorporated an improved blast fragmentation warhead that significantly increased the weapon's lethality.

B-52G 58-0170 of the 668th BMW, 416th BMW at Griffiss AFB was armed with AGM-86B missiles. The 416th BMW was the first SAC wing to become operational with ALCM. (Staff Sgt. Ernie Sealing / USAF)

The first lot of Block 1 CALCMs was delivered to the Air Force in July 1996, and all Block 0 missiles remaining in the inventory were upgraded to Block 1. Block 1 was further improved to produce the CALCM Block 1A. Block 1A included an eight-channel GPS receiver with navigation and guidance enhancements and an adaptive antenna array for precision delivery with a high degree of anti-jam immunity. To expand CALCM applications, an enhanced capability for shallow to near-vertical dive angles from any approach reference point also was implemented. The projected accuracy for the CALCM Block 1A was 3 meters including an estimated target-location error of two meters. The first operation Block 1A was delivered by Boeing to the U.S. Air Force in January 2001, and the first operational test launch was by the 93rd BS and 49th Test and Evaluation Squadron (TES) on 21 August 2001.

The AGM-86D CALCM Block 2 filled the requirement for a stand-off missile to attack deeply buried targets. The AGM-86D had a 1,000-pound penetration warhead to punch through to the target before detonation. The Block 2 missile was first flight tested in November 2002.

The Boeing AGM-86B was highly successful, but the U.S. Air Force desired an even more lethal cruise missile that fully employed low-observables (stealth) technology to stay ahead of Soviet defenses. Lockheed and General Dynamics-Convair competed for the ACM contract, and General Dynamics was the winner. The ACM was designated the AGM-129A. Like other stealth programs, such as the F-117A and B-2A, the AGM-129A program was highly classified. The AGM-129A presented a striking appearance, with its forward swept wings and faceted nose. The air intake and exhaust were designed to reduce the radar and infrared signature of the ACM. The AGM-129A used the same W80-1 thermonuclear warhead as the AGM-86B, but had a more advanced Williams International F112-WR-100 turbofan engine. As well as being nearly invulnerable to air defense systems, the AGM-129A had longer range and improved navigation accuracy compared to the AGM-86B.

General Dynamics delivered the first production ACM to the U.S. Air Force in 1990. With the end of the Cold War, production was terminated after only 460 missiles were produced, the last being delivered in 1993. Some ACMs were also manufactured by McDonnell Douglas. The ACM was carried externally on the B-52H, six on each SUU-72/A pylon. It was never integrated with the B-52G and did not fit on the CSRL. The AGM-129B variant was in development but cancelled. Details of it have never been declassified. The ACM was retired in 2008 as part of American force reductions to comply with the Moscow Treaty on Strategic Offensive Reductions that was signed on 24 May 2002.

An important aspect of the cruise missile program was the Follow-on Operational Test and Evaluation (FOT&E) program, conducted by the 49th TES. In the Combat Hammer (conventional missiles) and Combat Sledgehammer (nuclear missiles) programs, 49th TES selected several ALCM, CALCM, and ACM each year for testing. Technicians with the 49th TES replaced the warheads with instrumentation and range safety packages. Then they observed the operational units that actually loaded and launched the missiles. The FOT&E program verified stockpile reliability, procedures, and training, ensuring the effectiveness of the B-52H.

Munitions loaders of the 5th Aircraft Maintenance Squadron load an SUU-67/A pylon with six ALCM missiles onto a B-52H. A pylon with six missiles weighs approximately as much as a fully loaded F-16A fighter. (Technical Sgt. Lee A. Osberry Jr. / USAF)

An Airman transports an AGM-86C CALCM at RAF Fairford, United Kingdom, on 30 March 1999. B-52H 60-0051 *Appetite for Destruction II* of the 23rd BS, 5th BW was being prepared for a mission during Operation Allied Force. (Staff Sgt. Jim Howard / USAF)

The initial production missiles had rounded noses. Operational B-52Gs (but not B-52Hs) modified to carry the AGM-86B had a strakelet at the forward wing root, which can be compared to the test B-52G and the B-52H on page 38 that both lack the strakelet. (Technical Sgt. John L. Marine / USAF)

The AGM-86B later got the "Beluga whale" nose with a pronounced chine. The red covers were for the temperature probe on the left side of the missile and the pitot-static probe on the right side before flight. The radar altimeter antenna is located on the bottom of the missile. (Author)

The ALCM wings were stowed before launch. All flight surfaces deployed very quickly after launch to stabilize the missile, followed by engine start. The Remove Before Flight streamer to the left of the wing pivot points is for the safety pin that is inserted in the MAU-12D/A ejector rack. (Author)

When carried on the B-52, the vertical fin was folded to the left, the two elevons were folded upward, the engine inlet was stowed, and the engine exhaust nozzle was covered. After launch, the inlet, fin and elevons deployed and the engine exhaust nozzle cover was jettisoned. (Author)

This CSRL lacks MAU-12D/A ejector racks and has no weapons loaded on it. The view is from the forward part of the bomb bay, looking aft. At the top of the photograph is the hydraulic power drive unit that rotates the CSRL through 340 degrees. The cable reel for power and avionics signals is aft of the power drive unit. (Author)

The MHU-196/M trailer had a capacity of 40,000 pounds. It moved and lifted the CSRL loaded with 8 ALCMs. It could precisely position its load in all three dimensions. (Technical Sgt. Lee A. Osberry Jr. / USAF)

The spline at the front of the CSRL transmits torque from the hydraulic power drive unit to rotate the CSRL shaft. The cable reel holds the cables that supply electrical power and avionics commands to the CSRL electronics and the missiles. (U.S. Air Force photo Senior Airman Alexandra Longfellow / USAF)

As they do on the ALCM, the wings and tail of the ACM deploy immediately after launch. The faceted nose and unusual engine exhaust are features that decrease radar and infrared signatures. (USAF)

As well as loading an entire loaded pylon, cruise missiles can be loaded individually when the pylon is mounted on the airplane. (Author)

The SUU-72/A pylon carried six AGM-129A missiles, whose flying surfaces were folded prior to launch. (Staff Sgt. Jocelyn Rich / USAF)

The AGM-129A was tested in the McKinley Climatic Laboratory, Eglin AFB. It had three folding tail surfaces to provide control and stability in flight, and a low-observable engine exhaust. (Greg Murry / USAF)

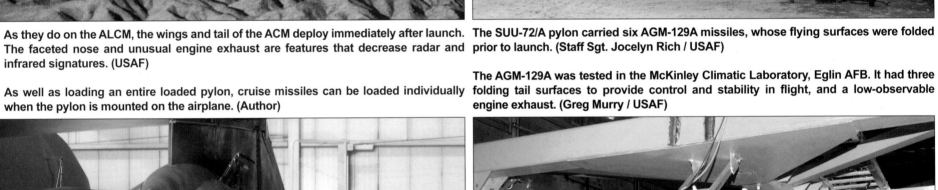

Conventional Weapons

Conventional Bombs

The B-52 first delivered conventional bombs in combat when 30 B-52F Stratofortresses of the 3960th Strategic Wing flew the first Arc Light mission from Andersen AFB, Guam, to South Vietnam on 18 June 1965. The B-52F and later the B-52D and B-52G primarily dropped the Mk 82 500-pound and M117 750-pound bombs in Southeast Asia.

The most common conventional weapons used by the B-52 were unguided general-purpose bombs. These weapons had a metal case with a high explosive filling and worked by blast and fragmentation effects. While these were the least expensive and least sophisticated weapons delivered by the B-52, they were effective against a wide variety of targets. Aside from the physical effects of the bombs, the psychological effect of a literal rain of destruction from an unseen bomber was devastating to enemy morale. Low-drag bombs were used for high-altitude delivery. Bombs with air inflatable retarders or retarding fins were used for low-altitude delivery to maximize aircraft separation distance from the bombs when they detonated. The B-52H could carry weapons on racks in the bomb bay and under each wing on a Heavy Stores Adapter Beam (HSAB) that was suspended from the stub pylon.

A cluster bomb consisted of a dispenser that opened after release at a preset altitude and spread submunitions over a wide area. The post-Vietnam-War family of cluster bombs all used the Tactical Munitions Dispenser (TMD). They were first used in Operation Desert Storm, after which they completely replaced earlier weapons. One limitation of cluster bombs is that if they were dropped from high altitude, winds could blow them away from the aimpoint during the long descent. To address this deficiency, Lockheed Martin developed the Wind Corrected Munitions Dispenser (WCMD), a guidance kit attached to the tail of the TMD. Using the OAS, the B-52 crew downloaded an aimpoint to the WCMD. After release, the guidance system compensated for wind and other sources of trajectory variation to guide the TMD to the point where it dispensed its bomblets.

The CBU-105/B Sensor Fuzed Weapons (SFW) were a specialized type of cluster bomb. The TMD with WCMD tail assembly dispensed 10 SFW munitions, each of which then launched four Skeet projectiles. The Skeet descended on parachutes, searching for vehicular targets with their sensors. After detecting a target, the Skeet fired an explosively forged penetrator into the thin top armor of the vehicle, likely destroying it. With each SFW delivering 40 Skeet, the SFW was an ideal weapon for attacking massed tanks.

Less well-known than the lethal bombs but occasionally used by the B-52H was the M129 leaflet bomb. One tactic was to include an M129 in a load of conventional bombs, advising the survivors of the attack to surrender before they are attacked again.

Sea mines were another type of B-52H munition.

The capability of the B-52H was dramatically improved by the integration of guided bombs. The Joint Direct Attack Munition (JDAM) was the principal guided bomb delivered by the B-52H. JDAM was a kit produced by Boeing that converted unguided free-fall bombs into smart bombs. The initial version of the JDAM was the GBU-

B-52H radar navigator Capt. Bryan "Squarebush" Roundtree shows the bomb bay to a visiting admiral. The B-52 bomb bay holds 27 Mk 82 bombs, nine each in forward, center, and aft cluster racks. (Senior Airman Rebecca M. Luquin / USAF)

Airman 1st Class Jason Stromberg straps down a live 750 pound M117 bomb onto a specialized bomb lift for loading on to a B-52H Stratofortress. (Staff Sgt. Vanessa Valentine / USAF)

Unguided Bombs

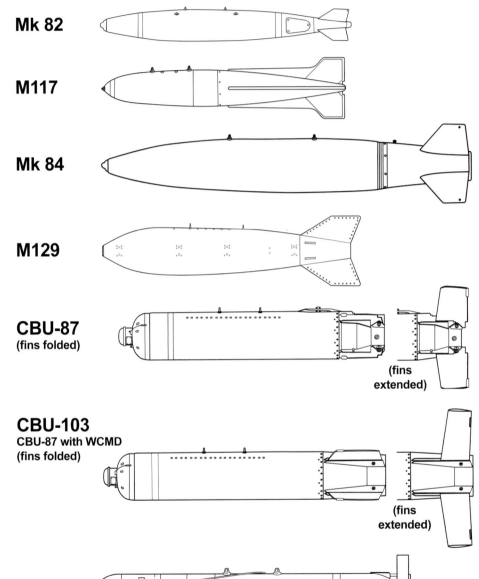

Mk 82

M117

Mk 84

M129

CBU-87
(fins folded)

(fins extended)

CBU-103
CBU-87 with WCMD
(fins folded)

(fins extended)

Mk 56

Airmen from the 36th Expeditionary Aircraft Maintenance Squadron load a Mk 56 sea mine onto a B-52H of the 23rd Expeditionary Bomb Squadron (EBS). (Staff Sgt. Eric Petosky / USAF)

Nine CBU-87/B cluster bombs can be carried by each HSAB. The CBU-87/B consists of an SUU-65/B Tactical Munitions Dispenser that contains 202 BLU-97/B Combined Effects Bomblets and an FZU-39/B proximity sensor. The BLU-97/B, effective against armor, personnel, and material, contains a shaped charge, scored steel casing, and zirconium ring for anti-armor, fragmentation, and incendiary capability. (Master Sgt. Travis Gregurek / USAF)

The M129 leaflet bomb can be carried in the bomb bay and on the HSAB. Each M129 contains tens of thousands of leaflets, which are dispensed when the M129 opens. (Master Sgt. Travis Gregurek / USAF)

Radar navigator Capt. Peter Terrebonne inspects a GBU-31(V)1/B. The Mk 84 bomb body is olive with a yellow band around the nose. The JDAM wings and tail kit are gray. Steel bands hold the wings on the bomb body. (Airman Tabitha Wininger / USAF)

31(V)1/B. This weapon consists of a Mk 84 2,000-pound class bomb body with strap-on airfoils and a KMU-556/B tail kit. The tail kit contained an inertial measurement unit, a GPS satellite navigation receiver, a guidance computer, and fin actuators. An alternative JDAM warhead to the Mk 84 was the BLU-109/B, a 2,000-pound class penetrating bomb intended to attack buried or fortified targets. The basic JDAM with BLU-109/B was designated the GBU-31(V)3/B with KMU-557/B tail kit. Yet another version of JDAM cleared for the B-52H in 2006 was the GBU-38/B, which used a Mk 82 500-pound class bomb instead of the larger Mk 84.

In operation, the B-52H OAS aligned the JDAM guidance system and downloaded target coordinates to it. Once released from the aircraft, the JDAM autonomously navigated to the designated target coordinates. The JDAM system provided a weapon circular error probable (CEP) of 13 meters or less during free flight when GPS data were available. If GPS data was denied, the JDAM would achieve a 30-meter CEP or less for free flight times up to 100 seconds. With the JDAM, the B-52H could attack single or multiple targets on a single pass. Each JDAM in a salvo could have a different target. Compared to laser-, television-, or infrared-guided weapons, JDAM was less accurate but was immune to the effects of degraded visibility. Therefore it could be delivered in any weather. The B-52H could carry six JDAMs on each HSAB, for a total of 12.

The B-52H achieved Initial Operational Capability (IOC) with JDAM on 5 December 2000, the first combat aircraft to do so. JDAM was an outstanding success in combat during Operations Enduring Freedom and Iraqi Freedom, launched from the B-52H and several other types of aircraft.

The stub pylon and HSAB allow the B-52H to carry up to nine stores under each wing, depending on the type of munition. (Author)

JDAMs (guided bombs)

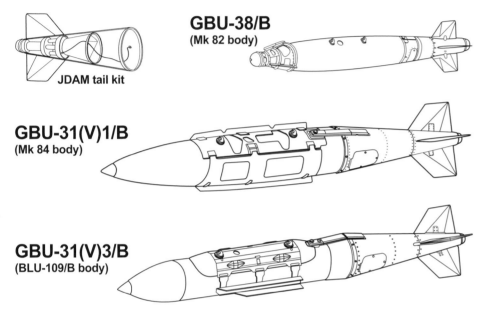

GBU-38/B
(Mk 82 body)

JDAM tail kit

GBU-31(V)1/B
(Mk 84 body)

GBU-31(V)3/B
(BLU-109/B body)

The Joint Direct Attack Munition (JDAM) was the guided weapon most commonly used by the B-52H during Operations Enduring Freedom and Iraqi Freedom. This munition is the GBU-31(V)3/B, which mates the JDAM wings and guidance tail kit to the BLU-109/B penetrator. The GBU-31(V)3/B proved to be a lethal weapon against caves, bunkers, and buried targets. (Staff Sgt. Jessica Kochman / USAF)

B-52H 60-0050, a heavily instrumented test aircraft assigned to the 419th Flight Test Squadron, Edwards AFB, delivers a weapon during flight testing of B-52H/JDAM integration. The first guided drop from a B-52H was conducted on 30 April 1997. In this test, the GBU-31(V)1/B was dropped at 20,000 feet and Mach 0.8. The target on the Naval Air Weapons Station (NAWS) China Lake range was 33,000 feet downrange, and the miss distance was 3.7 meters. (USAF)

Six JDAMs can be carried on each HSAB. These JDAMs are the GBU-31(V)1/B version, which uses the Mk 84 general-purpose bomb. (Senior Airman Rebecca M. Luquin / USAF)

In 2008, a B-52H delivered a GBU-54/B Laser JDAM for the first time during a test. The GBU-54/B was a GBU-38/B JDAM with an added DSU-38/B laser seeker that could acquire and track laser-designated targets. The additional targeting mode gave the B-52H crew the tactical flexibility of using either GPS or laser guidance modes.

The Boeing GBU-39/B Small Diameter Bomb (SDB) was essentially a miniature JDAM. Only 70.8 inches long, 7.5 inches wide, and 285 pounds, the SDB achieved a stand-off range of 60 nautical miles by gliding on wings that were deployed after release. The weapon was capable of penetrating more than 3 feet of steel-reinforced concrete. The small size and accuracy of SDB allowed the B-52H to attack more targets on a sortie with less collateral damage. Reducing collateral damage was important when providing close air support to friendly ground forces and when attacking targets in urban areas where civilians were likely to be close to targets. Four SDBs were carried on each BRU-61/A smart bomb rack. The BRU-61/A not only carried the SDB and separates it from the aircraft, but also interfaced the weapons with the avionics of the launch aircraft. The first operational launch aircraft for the SDB was the F-15E in October 2006, with the B-52H and other U.S. Air Force strike aircraft to follow.

Another B-52H weapon was the Paveway laser-guided bomb, which had previously only been used by fighters and attack aircraft. The B-52H could deliver a variety of laser-guided bombs, including the awesome GBU-28A/B with the BLU-113A/B "bunker buster." To deliver a laser-guided bomb, the target was illuminated by a Litening pod on the B-52H or a laser designator used by another aircraft or personnel on the ground. As

Several BRU-61/A smart carriage units can be mounted on each HSAB, and each BRU-61/A carries four Small Diameter Bombs (SDB). These SDB are painted orange, signifying test units. (USAF)

Small Diameter Bomb

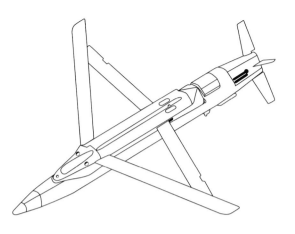

The GBU-39/B SDB is an advanced GPS/inertial guided 250-pound class bomb. It has wings that extend after launch to provide a longer stand-off range. The small size of the SDB is a benefit when collateral damage is a concern or when the B-52H is delivering weapons in close support of friendly troops. It also allows a large number of weapons to be carried. (USAF)

Laser-Guided Bombs

GBU-12
(Mk 82 body)

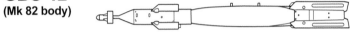

GBU-10
(Mk 84 body)

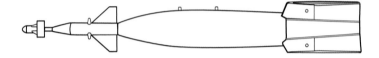

GBU-28
(BLU-113A/B body)

The GBU-28A/B is a 4,700-pound "bunker buster" that uses the BLU-113A/B penetrator and the Paveway III semiactive laser-homing guidance package. The B-52H can carry two GBU-28A/B bombs on each HSAB. The B-52H has never used this weapon in combat. (Author)

Aircrew members perform a preflight inspection of GBU-12D/B Paveway II laser-guided bombs before their first combat delivery by a B-52H during Operation Iraqi Freedom (OIF). (Airman 1st Class Stacia M. Willis / USAF)

of 2006, the only combat use of laser-guided bombs from the B-52H was on one mission during Operation Iraqi Freedom, when the GBU-12D/B Paveway II was used. The GBU-12D/B was a laser-guided version of the Mk 82 bomb. The great tactical advantage of laser-guided bombs was their high accuracy against point targets. This advantage was traded against the complexity of coordinating weapon delivery with laser designation and the inability of laser-guided bombs to function in degraded visual conditions, including fog, smoke, dust, and clouds.

Conventional Missiles

The range, payload, and offensive avionics of the B-52 made it an ideal platform for launching missiles. Missiles, in turn, allowed the B-52, which had neither exceptional speed nor low observables, to be a viable weapon system in high-threat environments by standing off outside the range of enemy air defense systems.

In response to the expanding Soviet navy, the McDonnell Douglas (now Boeing) AGM-84 Harpoon anti-ship cruise missile was the first conventional missile integrated with the B-52. It weighed 1,145 pounds and was 12 feet 7 inches long. Powered by a Teledyne J402-CA-400 turbojet engine to provide a range in excess of 60 nautical miles, the AGM-84 Harpoon used an inertial guidance system until the active radar seeker was turned on and locked onto a target. The Harpoon could fly at sea-skimming altitudes to evade defenses, then make a terminal area pop-up and dive into the target ship. The 488-pound WDU-18/B penetrating blast-fragmentation warhead was detonated by a time-delayed impact fuze.

The Harpoon and the AN/AWG-19 Harpoon Air Launch Control Set (HALCS) were first integrated with a B-52G in March 1983. Four AGM-84 missiles could be carried on each HSAB. Three successful test launches led to the modification of a total of 30 non-ALCM B-52Gs with HALCS, enough to provide two squadrons of Harpoon-capable B-52Gs by 30 June 1985. The 42nd BW at Loring AFB, Maine, and the 43rd BW at Andersen AFB, Guam, performed the Harpoon mission.

After the retirement of the B-52Gs with HALCS in May 1994, the Harpoon mission was moved to the 2nd BW at Barksdale AFB. Four B-52H models were modified as an interim measure to accept HALCS. Eventually, HALCS was removed, and the AGM-84 Harpoon missiles were targeted and launched by the Harpoon SMO in the OAS, giving all B-52Hs a Harpoon capability by 1997. With the absence of a major blue-water threat, the ACC retired the Harpoon from the B-52H arsenal in 2004 to simplify training and logistics.

During the Cold War, the American airpower professionals feared the Soviet integrated air defense system, with its interlocking radars, command centers, missiles, and guns. The high loss rate suffered by American aircraft over North Vietnam was a painful experience, and the serious damage inflicted on the Israeli Air Force in 1973 by the Soviet-equipped air defenses of Egypt and Syria confirmed the threat.

One of the less well-known efforts to handle this threat was the Northrop AGM-136A Tacit Rainbow. Tacit Rainbow was a low-cost missile that could autonomously locate and neutralize enemy air defense radars. The operational concept was for B-52G bombers or fighter/attack aircraft to launch a large number of Tacit Rainbows toward

B-52G 58-0202 waits on the ramp at Mather AFB, California, for the first launch of an AGM-84 Harpoon from a B-52 on 14 March 1983. (USAF)

AGM-84 Harpoon

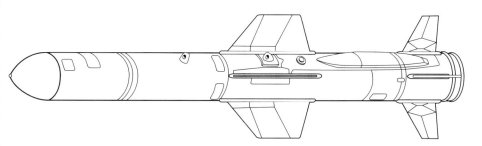

enemy air defense systems. After launch, each missile would deploy flying surfaces and start its engine. It would fly along its programmed flight path until it detected radar that matched the parameters in its target data file. Then, the missile would attack the radar. If the enemy chose to turn off the radar to protect it from the Tacit Rainbow, then the friendly strike aircraft could penetrate undetected.

Tacit Rainbow was propelled by a Williams International F121-WR-100 turbofan engine. The engine, the composite airframe, and the electronics used innovative technologies to achieve a low unit cost, which was essential to the operational concept that envisaged large numbers of Tacit Rainbows being launched to saturate enemy defenses. The passive sensor determined the specific types of radars that it detected, and the autonomous guidance logic allowed the missile to counter a variety of defensive tactics used by radar operators.

The B-52G could carry Tacit Rainbows on a rotary launcher in the bomb bay. The launcher was specially designed for the Tacit Rainbow and used only for it. It carried the 30 missiles in three rows of 10 and occupied the entire bomb bay. The B-52G crew used the OAS with the Tacit Rainbow SMO to apply power to the missiles, load mission data,

An AGM-136A Tacit Rainbow missile flies over NWC China Lake. The test missiles were painted orange with a gray radome. The black and white markings aided visual tracking. (Capt. Walter F. Davidson / USAF)

A B-52G from the Guam-based 60th Bombardment Squadron (BMS), 43rd Bombardment Wing (BMW), carries a single AGM-84 Harpoon missile on a stub pylon and HSAB under its left wing in 1990. (Chief Master Sgt. Don Sutherland / USAF)

control the rotary launcher, and command launches.

In 1984-85, the Tacit Rainbow concept was first validated in a series of highly classified "black" flight tests launched from A-7 Corsair II and C-130 Hercules airplanes. With the concept validated, the definitive missile was then designed. Flight tests of this design commenced in 1987 from Edwards AFB, California. On 20 March, 17 April, and 29 April of that year, inert Tacit Rainbow jettison test vehicles were dropped from B-52G 57-6519 to verify separation dynamics. The remainder of 1987 was used for captive carry tests under the wing of a Navy A-6E Intruder, with the engine operating.

The first free flight was a launch from an A-6E Intruder on 3 November 1987, which resulted in a crash when the tail did not deploy after launch. The first successful flight was achieved on 12 April 1988, also from an A-6E. The first launch from a B-52 was on 10 January 1989. Although the Tacit Rainbow was intended for the B-52G, a B-52H (60-0050, call sign "Torch 01," assigned to the 6519th Test Squadron) was used for this and subsequent test launches because of test aircraft availability. The flight test program had a mixed record. With the end of the Cold War, the military budget was slashed, and the Tacit Rainbow program was terminated in 1992.

Another "black" program was the Northrop AGM-137A Tri-Service Surface Attack Missile (TSSAM). TSSAM was intended for non-ALCM B-52Gs, with six carried externally on each HSAB. TSSAM was 14 feet long and weighed approximately 2,000 pounds. It had a Williams International F122-WR-100 turbofan engine, inertial/GPS *en route* guidance, imaging infrared (IIR) terminal guidance, very low observables, and a conventional warhead.

Armed with 12 TSSAMs and 30 Tacit Rainbows, the B-52G would have been the ultimate conventional deep strike platform of the era. But TSSAM was cancelled in December 1994 because of cost and technical problems.

While TSSAM was being developed, SAC wanted an interim stand-off precision conventional weapon for the B-52G. The U.S. Air Force chose the Popeye missile from Rafael Armament Development Authority of Israel to meet the requirement. In U.S. Air Force service, the Popeye was known as the AGM-142 Have Nap. On the B-52G, the complete Have Nap system consisted of two missiles in tandem on the left HSAB, one missile forward and the AN/ASW-55 datalink pod aft on the right HSAB, and the AGWCP at the radar navigator's crew station. Only a few B-52Gs were modified for Have Nap, and only six radar navigators at a time were kept qualified in the weapon system.

The AGM-142 missile was 15 feet, 10 inches long and weighed 3,000 pounds. It had a solid-fuel rocket engine that gave it a range of 50 miles. *En route* guidance was inertial. The AGM-142A and AGM-142C models had TV terminal guidance, while the AGM-142B and AGM-142D had IIR. The AGM-142A and AGM-142B used a blast/fragmentation warhead, while the AGM-142C and AGM-142D used a penetrating warhead.

In operation, the crew programmed the waypoints of the trajectory into the missile. Like ALCM and ACM, a good transfer alignment was critical because a poorly aligned INS would not place the missile in a position where the TV or IIR could be used for the terminal engagement.

AGM-137A TSSAM

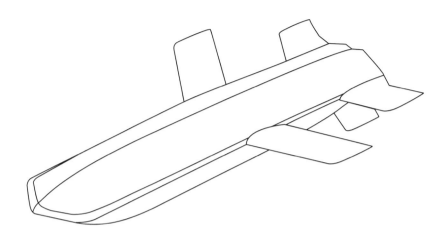

In contrast to the exotic and troublesome TSSAM, the AGM-142 Have Nap was a low-risk program that used the Popeye missile from Israel. The AGM-142 was initially used by the B-52G and later by the B-52H after the B-52G was retired. (Lockheed Martin)

A pair of AGM-142 Have Nap missiles hang on an HSAB attached to a stub pylon under the left wing of B-52G 57-6520 of the 34th BS. The missiles are light gray, and the red protective covers for the sensor windows are removed before flight. The blue bands signify that these are inert missiles. (Brian Lockett)

The right stub pylon and HSAB of B-52G 57-6520 carries an AN/ASW-55 data link pod for Have Nap. It was on display at the 24 October 1993 Open House at Castle AFB, California. (Brian Lockett)

The rocket motor ignited after the missile dropped clear of the B-52. Normally, the missile flew on autopilot to the vicinity of the target and transmitted TV or IIR imagery, which was received by the datalink pod and displayed on the AGWCP. At any point in the flight, the radar navigator could take control by datalink through the AGWCP and fly the missile manually using the seeker imagery. As the missile approached the target, the radar navigator identified the target, locked the missile seeker on it, and then enabled automatic terminal guidance, which could be manually overridden at any time. Clouds, smoke, or other degraded visual conditions in the target area could hinder effective employment of Have Nap.

In 1992, Have Nap capabilities were concentrated in the 34th BS, 366th WG. With the retirement of the B-52G and the conversion of the 34th BS to the B-1B Lancer, a few B-52Hs of the 2nd BW were modified for Have Nap. Have Nap was retired in 2004.

Another guided weapon integrated with the B-52H was the Raytheon AGM-154A Joint Stand-Off Weapon (JSOW), a GPS-guided weapon dispensing BLU-97/B bomblets. An SMO for JSOW was developed, and JSOW was flight tested from the B-52H. The U.S. Air Force, however, did not deploy it operationally on the B-52H.

In the aftermath of the TSSAM cancellation, the U.S. Air Force initiated the Joint Air-to-Surface Standoff Missile (JASSM) program to satisfy the requirement for a missile to attack heavily defended targets from stand-off ranges. The Lockheed Martin AGM-158A competed against the McDonnell Douglas (later Boeing) AGM-159A for the JASSM contract, and the AGM-158A was selected in April 1998. The AGM-158A utilized a Teledyne J402-CA-100 turbojet engine,

AGM-142 Have Nap

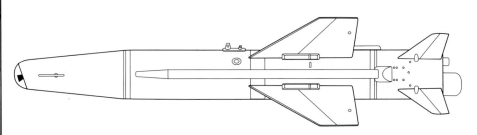

B-52H 60-0050 of the 419th Flight Test Squadron, 412th Test Wing, releases an AGM-154A Joint Stand-Off Weapon (JSOW). The test took place on 8 February 2002, and two JSOWs were released at 35,000 feet and Mach 0.8. (Bobbi Garcia / USAF)

Each HSAB can carry six AGM-158A missiles, for a total load of 12 on each B-52H. This HSAB is loaded with inert Joint Air-to-Surface Standoff Missile (JASSM) shapes that are used for training munitions load crews. (USAF)

AGM-154A JSOW & AGM-158A JASSM

A high-speed camera at the White Sands Missile Range captures the phenomenal terminal accuracy demonstrated by a JASSM during a developmental flight test. This photograph was retouched to obscure classified features. (USAF / Lockheed Martin)

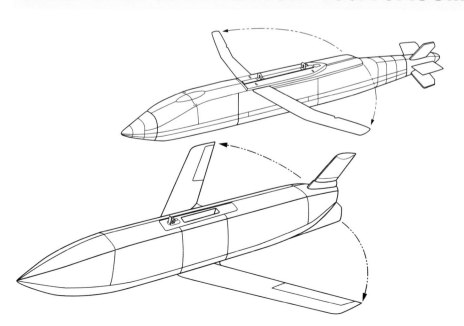

The B-52H carried nine MALD vehicles on each HSAB, in forward, middle and aft triplets. (Raytheon)

The grid stability augmentation device on the aft end stabilized the decoy after launch. (Raytheon)

GPS/inertial *en route* guidance, and an IIR seeker with autonomous target recognition capability. The AGM-158A weighed 2,250 pounds and was 14 feet long. Six JASSM could be carried on each HSAB, for a total of 12 per B-52H. The shape and materials of the AGM-158A were driven by low-observables considerations. JASSM had a 1,000-pound WDU-42/B penetrating warhead and a range of 200 miles.

The first powered flight test of the AGM-158A was on 20 November 1999. Several test failures delayed the program. The AGM-158A was ready for operational use on the B-52H and B-2A in October 2003. In May 2004, the Air Force approved full-rate production of the AGM-158A. The AGM-158A was also employed with the B-1B, F-16C/D, and F/A-18E/F.

The JASSM-ER (Extended Range) was a 500-mile-range version of the AGM-158A and was designated AGM-158B. It was powered by the Williams International F107-WR-105 turbofan. The first test launch of an AGM-158B was on 18 May 2006, from a B-1B flying over the White Sands Missile Range, New Mexico. JASSM-ER is planned to enter service in 2013.

Miniature Air-Launched Decoy

The ADM-160 Miniature Air-Launched Decoy (MALD) was an expendable decoy, with the same role as the ADM-20 Quail and the SCAD that was the predecessor to the ALCM. In 1995, the Defense Advanced Research Project Agency initiated the MALD program, with an emphasis on affordability. A year later, Teledyne Ryan (later Northrop Grumman) won the contract to develop MALD, which was designated ADM-160A. The ADM-160A first flew on 9 January 1999, launched from an F-16. In the end, the USAF decided not to put the ADM-160A into production, judging that its range was inadequate for the mission.

The MALD® (a registered trademark of Raytheon Company) program was revived in 2003, with Raytheon as the prime contractor for the ADM-160B, a larger vehicle with longer range than the ADM-160A. The ADM-160B was a 280-pound vehicle with a Hamilton Sundstrand TJ-150 turbojet engine. The payload of the ADM-160B was an active radar signature enhancer, making it appear to radars as a strike aircraft. The first powered flight of the ADM-160B was on 13 June 2007, launched from an F-16. Later flight tests included launches from a B-52H. Raytheon began production deliveries in 2009 and the ADM-160B became operational in 2011.

The ADM-160B was launched from the B-52H in a similar manner to other missiles such as ALCM, ACM, and JASSM. Using OAS running the MALD SMO, the navigator tested the vehicle, downloaded the mission data to it and conducted a transfer alignment of its navigation system. After launch, a grid stability augmentation device stabilized the MALD vehicle during separation from the B-52H. Then the vehicle jettisoned the grid stability augmentation device and started its engine, after which it followed a programmed flight plan. With its flight profile and radar signature mimicking a combat aircraft, the ADM-160B was intended to deceive enemy air defense systems and divert their attention from the actual strike aircraft.

Depending on the specific tactics employed, the MALD vehicles might be used to draw air defense forces away from the strike force, lure the enemy into turning on surface-to-air missile guidance radars which would reveal their position for subsequent destruction, or absorb surface-to-air missiles so that the missile launchers are empty when the strike force comes into range of them.

The ADM-160C MALD-J was the next version of the MALD vehicle. The ADM-160C was equipped with a radar jammer payload and retained the decoy function as well. The ADM-160C had its first free flight on 9 December 2009 from an F-16 and was first launched from a B-52H on 4 May 2011.

Massive Ordnance Penetrator

With rogue nations such as North Korea and Iran unable to deploy air defenses capable of stopping an American or allied air attack against their nuclear weapons capabilities, they moved to a strategy of placing key facilities in deep underground bunkers. Protected by hundreds of feet of soil and rock, the facilities were invulnerable to penetrating munitions such as the BLU-109/B and even the BLU-113A/B. Nuclear bombs such as the B53 and B61-11 could destroy these targets, but the use of nuclear weapons would be problematic in many scenarios. This situation led the Defense Threat Reduction Agency to develop the GBU-57A/B Massive Ordnance Penetrator (MOP), a 30,000-pound conventional penetrating weapon. Dropped from high altitude, the MOP would use its immense mass, velocity and hardened body to smash through rock and soil, delivering several tons of high explosives deep underground.

The MOP was intended to arm the B-2A Spirit. However, the B-52H was used as the delivery vehicle during the technology demonstration phase of the project, which had five MOP drops that ended in 2009.

Senior Airman Jason Sperry, 917th Aircraft Maintenance Squadron, prepares to use an MJ-1 munitions lift truck to hoist an ADM-160B up to the HSAB as Senior Airman James Hudson, 917th Aircraft Maintenance Squadron, connects the MJ-1 to the vehicle. The grid stability augmentation device has two safety pins with red Remove Before Flight streamers. (Senior Airman Alexandra M. Longfellow / USAF)

B-52H 60-0050 releases a GBU-57A/B Massive Ordnance Penetrator (MOP) during a test of the weapon over White Sands Missile Range in 2009. (Defense Threat Reduction Agency)

The umbilical provided power to the vehicle before launch and interfaced it to the OAS. (Raytheon)

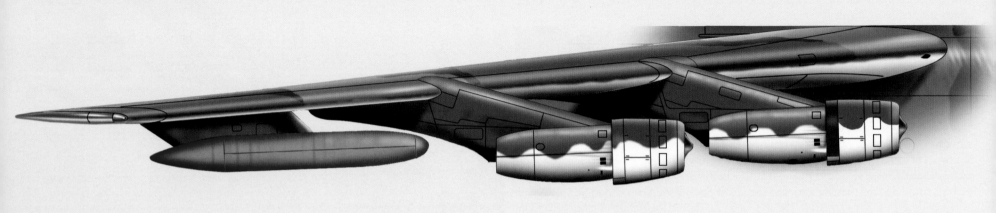

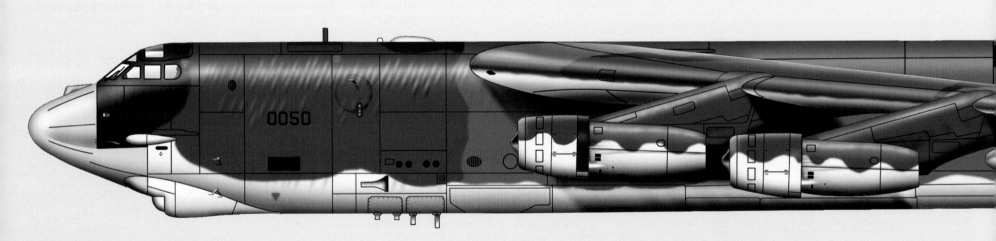

0050

B-52H 60-0050 was with the 6519th Test Squadron, 6512th Test Wing, at Edwards AFB in 1989. This aircraft was one of the last B-52s to wear the Strategic Integrated Operational Plan (SIOP) camouflage and at the time was serving as the test platform for the AGM-136A Tacit Rainbow missile. The right tip tank was painted orange and modified to be a camera pod for documenting missile separation.

Flying the BUFF

Before flying in the B-52H, I attended a two-day aerospace physiology course at Peterson AFB. The day before the flight, I took egress (ejection and bailout) training provided by instructors of the 5th Operations Support Squadron, 5th BW. After training, I proceeded to the 23rd BS, 5th BW, to meet my crew and attend the mission briefing. The aircraft commander was Capt. Andrew J. Bemis, with the other crewmembers being co-pilot 1st Lt. Richard H. Waters IV, radar navigator Capt. Jonathan W. Beich, navigator 1st Lt. Scott E. Axelson, and electronic warfare officer (EWO) 1st Lt. Jeffrey M. Simonds. Bemis and Beich were combat veterans, and the three lieutenants were recent graduates of flight training.

The briefing covered a two-ship training mission. Our sortie was assigned the call sign "Chill 25," and the lead aircraft was "Chill 24." The highlights of the mission would be aerial refueling and simulated weapon delivery.

The next morning, the two crews met at 0930L (local time) for a weather briefing and some words from the squadron operations officer. Recently, a Minot B-52 had hit a truck with its wing tip while taxiing. The wings of the B-52 are long and swept, and from the cockpit the pilots have little visibility of the wing tips. The operations officer cautioned us to stop and request a ground spotter if there was any doubt about obstructions. Then the two crews boarded the bus to the flight line.

As we crossed onto the flight line, the mission commander called out "rings, rags, and tags," meaning that the crewmembers should remove rings, scarves, and patches to deny intelligence to the enemy if the airplane were shot down. This seemed an unlikely event — the target was in South Dakota — but as the saying goes, "train the way that you fight." Arriving at our airplane, B-52H 60-0033 *Instrument of Destruction,* we left the bus and began preflight activities. A "cocked" airplane with a nearby crew on alert could get off the ground in minutes, but a routine flight required approximately an hour and a half of preparation between the arrival of the crew and the takeoff. Even before the aircrew arrived, the crew chiefs had their own extensive checklist to work through. First, the aircrew did a walk-around inspection, with each member assigned to a different part of the airplane. Then the aircrew met with crew chiefs to review the aircraft maintenance paperwork.

The aircrew boarded the B-52 through a hatch in the belly of the aircraft, aft of the navigators' stations. The two navigators then moved forward to their downward-firing ejection seats. The others climbed up a short ladder on the right side of the cockpit behind the navigators' seats to the upper deck, with the pilots going forward and the EWO going backward to their respective crew stations. Four upward-firing ejection seats were on the upper level of the cockpit, two for pilots and two rearward-facing seats at the back of the upper level for the EWO and gunner. Crews no longer had gunners, but the ejection seat remained. I first checked out the parachute at the instructor pilot seat in the space behind the two pilot ejection seats. Since the instructor pilot seat was not an ejection seat, in the event of a bailout I would have to egress the aircraft by moving to the lower level and exiting the aircraft through the opening left by the navigator's ejection seat

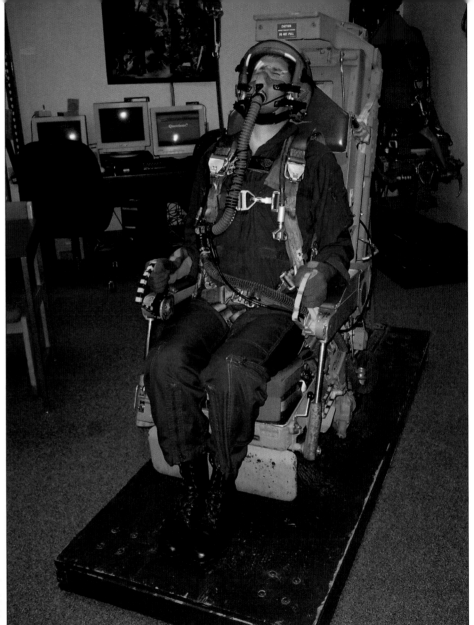

Arming levers – rotate. Trigger – squeeze! Attending aircraft egress training is a prerequisite to flying in the B-52. The parachutes are attached to the ejection seats. After verifying that the safety pins are inserted, the crewmember puts his arms through the arm straps, secures the groin straps and chest straps, and then fastens the lapbelt. In the picture, the author is in an upward-firing ejection seat. The radar navigator and navigator on the lower deck use downward-firing ejection seats, which differ in having a trigger ring between the legs and leg restraints that prevent the lower legs from flailing upward as the seats depart the aircraft. (Staff Sgt. Steven R. Grever / USAF)

after he ejected. It would be nice to have another option in this unlikely circumstance, so I also did a preflight inspection of the gunner's ejection seat.

While running the checklist before starting engines, the pilots found a problem with the flight controls, and the navigators had a problem with OAS. The "Chill 24" crew also had problems with their airplane. After both aircraft commanders consulted with squadron operations, we got approved to go to the spare aircraft. "Chill 24" would have to wait for another day. Our crew quickly packed up our gear and got a ride to the spare B-52H, 60-0060 *Iron Butterfly*. At the new airplane, we repeated the entire process of getting ready for engine start. The fuel totalizer gauge showed a load of 198,800 pounds.

Pilot: "Ground, start external air." The B-52H required an external source of pressurized air to start the engines because it did not have an internal auxiliary power unit. The ground crew had previously connected a pneumatic cart to the No. 4 engine (the engines were numbered Nos. 1-8, from left to right) and now they started the compressor on the cart.

Pilot: "Standby for engine start."
Radar navigator: "Offense ready."
EWO: "Defense ready."
Pilot: "Clear left."
Co-pilot: "Clear right."
Crew chief: "Clear on ground." With visibility to the engine pods from the cockpit being limited, it was essential for safety that the crew chief on the ground verified that the danger zones ahead of and behind the engines were clear of personnel and equipment.

The pilot started engine No. 4 at 1318L. Engine No. 4 crossfed the compressed air used to start engine No. 5 on the right side. With both engines running, the pilot directed the crew chiefs to disconnect the pneumatic cart. The pilots ran up engines No. 4 and No. 5 to 82 percent to increase the flow and pressure from the hydraulic pumps mounted on those engines for stabilizer checks. During the checks, the pilots compared the yoke and trim wheel positions with what the crew chief saw on the actual control surface, which was not visible to the pilots. Then the pilot set pitch trim for takeoff. It was critical to set pitch trim correctly since the B-52H elevator did not have sufficient pitch control authority to overpower the trim. An incorrect pitch trim setting could put the aircraft out of control after takeoff, with catastrophic results. At 1320L, the pilots ran up engines No. 4 and No. 5 to start the other engines with engine air bleed crossflow. They then started engines No. 1, No. 2, No. 3, No. 6, No. 7, and No. 8 simultaneously. The crew chief called out, "Eight good starts," and the navigator closed and locked the hatch.

At this point, the radar navigator reported that the OAS radar scan converter was not working and sent for a bomb/navigation system technician. While waiting for the technician, the pilots checked the engine anti-ice system by first running up engines No. 1, No. 2, No. 7, and No. 8 (the outboard engine pods), throttled back those four to idle, then repeated with engines No. 3, No. 4, No. 5, and No. 6 (the inboard engine pods). One benefit of the high complexity of the B-52 was tremendous redundancy, which enabled it to accomplish the mission even if there were failures or combat damage.

When the technician arrived, the pilot opened his sliding window to relieve the pressurization in the cockpit so that when the navigator opened the hatch, it would not swing open explosively and injure somebody. The technician cleared the OAS radar scan converter fault and then departed, but he returned in a few minutes when there was trouble operating the bomb bay doors. The pilot could manually open and close the doors, but the OAS could not. For the next half hour, with the engines consuming 8,000 pounds of fuel per hour at the idle power setting, the crew and technician tried to resolve the problem to no effect. Finally, they just decided to live with the problem, the bomb bay doors not being a real issue on a flight with only simulated weapons delivery.

At 1405L, we received our departure clearance: "'Chill 25,' cleared to Minot Air Force Base. After takeoff, fly runway heading, climb to Flight Level 230, expect Flight Level 350 in 10 minutes. Departure on Local Channel 4, squawk 7013." The tower reported variable winds at 5 knots, visibility of 7 miles, a broken ceiling 900 feet above ground level and overcast at 3,000 feet above ground level. At a gross weight of 394,000 pounds, lighter than the B-52H maximum gross weight of 488,000 pounds, we began to taxi after a brake check.

With a wingspan of 185 feet, the B-52H required taxiways and runways that are at least 200 feet wide; the runway at Minot AFB was 300 feet wide. The crosswind crab feature of the B-52 quadricycle landing gear could be preset and turned up to 20 degrees left or right of center during the approach. The maximum of 20 degrees crab accommodates landings in crosswinds up to and including 43 knots blowing up to 90 degrees to the runway at a landing weight of 270,000 pounds. While taxiing, the pilots checked the crosswind crab landing gear: left deflection, centered; right deflection, centered. This created the odd sensation of the aircraft pointing in a different direction than the direction of travel on the

From left are the author, Captain Beich, 1st Lt. Axelson, 1st Lt. Simonds, 1st Lt. Waters, and Capt. Bemis. B-52H 60-0033 *Instrument of Destruction* is still wearing its OIF mission markings in 2004. Because of mechanical problems, the crew switched to another aircraft before takeoff. (Unknown USAF crew chief)

B-52H 60-0060 *Iron Butterfly* was the spare aircraft used after 60-0033 broke. This aircraft still has its OIF mission markings. CALCM silhouettes are on the left, and bomb silhouettes are on the right. The outline of North Dakota to the right of the mission markings contains the name of the crew chief. (Author)

Two crew chiefs attach a compressed air hose from a starter cart to the No. 4 engine (inboard engine of the inboard pod on the left wing). Although the TF33-P-3 engines can be fitted with pyrotechnic start cartridges on alert, normal engine starts require ground support equipment. (Author)

ground. Another odd sensation was caused by the fact that the pilots sit approximately 35 feet ahead of the forward landing gear, so from their station it appeared that the airplane always overshot on turns when taxiing. Before requesting takeoff clearance, the pilot conducted final checks to ensure that the flight controls moved freely and were clear of obstructions, while the co-pilot configured the fuel system for takeoff.

Takeoff with the co-pilot at the controls was at 1425L. There was a calculated S1 (decision speed) of 111 KIAS (knots indicated airspeed) and an acceleration time to S1 of 15.3 seconds. If the aircraft hadn't attained a speed of at least 111 KIAS in 15.3 seconds, the pilot would have aborted the takeoff by moving the throttles to idle and slowing the airplane with ground brakes, spoilers (air brakes), and the drag chute.

For this flight, the S2 speed was 144 KIAS. S2 was unstick speed, the speed at which the pilot used back stick pressure to ensure the forward gear lifted off first. Since the B-52 was designed to drop bombs from high altitude, the wings had a 6-degree incidence angle relative to the fuselage. This allowed a level platform for weapon release. So if the pilot just let the B-52 lift up on its own, the forward gear would be on the ground with the aft gear in the air. This could lead to an over-control problem. The pilot not flying called 10 KIAS before S2 so that the pilot flying could start pulling the yoke back to ensure the forward gear lifted off first. After achieving S2, the next speed for which the pilots aimed was Minimum Speed for Direction Control (MSDC), which is calculated based on losing two outboard engines. This speed was always higher than S2 and increased with higher gross weights and air temperatures.

The initial climb was at 180 KIAS, and the flaps were retracted at 1,000 feet above ground level. The pilots cycled the aerial refueling slipway doors. If water leaked inside the doors, it could freeze at a high altitude and jam the doors. Opening the doors blew out any accumulated water. The navigator announced to the pilots that the OAS was supplying a good Flight Control Indicator (FCI), which was displayed on the EVS displays and provided course guidance to the pilots. At 12,000 feet, each member of the crew checked his oxygen equipment. Since the B-52 had a pressurized cockpit, the pilot cleared the crew to remove oxygen masks after the oxygen check was completed. After leveling off, the crew removed their helmets and put on headsets. Headsets were more comfortable than the helmets for long flights, although helmets were required to be worn when moving around the cockpit and during certain critical phases of flight.

During the flight, it was apparent that the B-52 fuel system, which was complex and manually controlled, was a major workload item for the co-pilot. The co-pilot acted as flight engineer and operated the fuel system control panel that faced him. The fuel sequence varied depending on the weapon load. The aircraft had a Center of Gravity/Fuel Level Advisory System (CG/FLAS) that aided the co-pilot in performing this task.

Fourteen minutes after takeoff, we passed through Flight Level 180, with our engines each consuming 3,400 pounds of fuel per hour. Meanwhile, the radar navigator and navigator were busy replanning the flight. With our delayed takeoff, it took some rearranging of the flight plan to make the aerial refueling control point and range times. This change meant that we would do aerial refueling before rather than after weapons delivery.

At Flight Level 290, the pilots established a level cruise at 0.755 Mach and fuel burn of 2,500 pounds per hour per engine. I put on my helmet and moved downstairs to join them.

The navigators sat in a windowless compartment, each facing two Multi-Function Displays (MFDs) and the other OAS controls. They had configured the OAS to simultaneously calculate three estimates of the aircraft position and speed, called INS1, INS2, and ALTER. The estimate for Inertial Navigation System 1 (INS1) used the GPS to correct for INS1 drift. The estimate for INS2 used the Doppler navigation radar instead of GPS to correct for INS2 drift. By not using GPS for one estimate, there was an independent check on GPS and a good navigation estimate even if GPS proved faulty. The ALTER (alternative) navigation solution was provided by the Attitude and Heading Reference System (AHRS) with GPS input. At 1541L, one of three OAS processors failed, but the OAS was redundant and reconfigured itself, so this had no effect on the mission.

For aerial refueling, the crew needed to be strapped in with helmets and oxygen masks on, and I returned to the instructor pilot seat. By 1549L, we were at the IP (initial point) for the AR106HE aerial refueling track. The co-pilot configured the fuel system for aerial refueling, opened the slipway doors, and turned on lights so that the tanker crew could see us more easily. The tanker, KC-135R 63-7999 from the 319th Aerial Refueling Wing, had the call sign "Raid 23." Over the radio, "Raid 23" told us it had a problem with its refueling boom, so we would only be able to fly in the precontact position.

"Raid 23" appeared one mile ahead of us, going 275 KIAS. We were 1,000 feet lower and going 290 KIAS, decelerating as we climbed and closed the distance. "Raid 23" cleared us for precontact, and we moved into position. The pilots took turns flying the B-52 in precontact, maintaining position relative to the tanker by looking through the "eyebrow" windows above the windshield. They positioned the B-52 so certain parts of the tanker were visible through certain parts of the windows. The pilots used many references to position themselves behind the tanker: inboard and outboard tanker engines, boom pod window, antenna, and rivet lines. The location and relative movement of these references in the windows provided indications for the pilots to make throttle adjustments and pitch/roll changes. The downwash from the tanker forced back the B-52H, and the pilots had to compensate. The pilots made frequent small control movements, often several times a second. This was an impressive display of airmanship – two big jets flying in close formation while maintaining relative position with an accuracy of a few feet. The normal procedure was for the KC-135R to refuel with its autopilot on, but next we practiced with the tanker autopilot turned off. With the autopilot off, the tanker was less stable, increasing the workload of both the KC-135R boom operator and the B-52H pilots.

We then practiced an emergency separation. The objective of emergency separation was to rapidly separate the tanker and receiver, while ensuring that they do not collide. At the call "break away, break away, break away," the KC-135R accelerated. The B-52H descended and decelerated. With aerial refueling complete, I moved downstairs to watch the navigators prepare for weapon delivery.

At 1635L, the navigators began the missile power application checklist for the

Guests of the BUFF sit in the instructor pilot seat behind the pilot and co-pilot. This position is not an ejection seat, and the occupant wears a parachute pack. The passenger is wearing an HGU-55/P helmet with a neutral gray polycarbonate visor. (1st Lt. Richard Waters / USAF)

The video display in front of the co-pilot was installed as part of the EVS upgrade in the 1970s. It is used to display EVS imagery as well as terrain avoidance guidance from the radar. More recently, a moving map format driven by OAS was added to the display options. The pilot also has a video display. (Author)

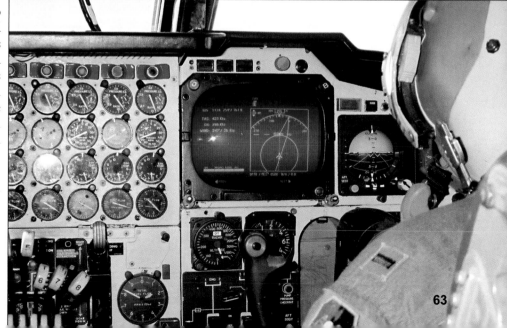

Radar navigator Capt. Beich leads the offensive team on the lower deck. (Author)

Navigator 1st Lt. Axelson enters data into the OAS using a keyboard. (Author)

CALCM. The navigator loaded the CALCM SMO software in the OAS processors. For our missile training exercise, the OAS was in FULL SIM (full simulation) mode; in any case we weren't actually carrying any CALCMs. The first step in missile power application was to apply power to the (simulated) Missile Interface Unit (MIU). Had we been using real missiles, the OAS would have been in STRIKE mode and the navigator would have applied MIU power at least 40 minutes before missile power application to allow the missile INS to warm up completely to maximize accuracy. In training without real missiles, this could be overridden for mission timing constraints. The next step was to power up the (simulated) missiles. On an OAS MFD, the navigators monitored the missiles as they powered up in Coarse Alignment (CA) mode and Safed (SAF).

The actual execution of the transfer alignment between the OAS and the CALCM INS was totally automated, with the OAS comparing the state vector from the CALCM INS with the state vector from the OAS and updating the CALCM INS to reduce the differences. While the transfer alignment was under way, the OAS also began to download the mission data to the CALCMs. Each missile could simultaneously carry up to three different mission data loads. With that capability, if a missile designated for a higher priority target failed, then a missile targeted as a lower priority target could be quickly retargeted before launch to the higher priority target. Using OAS, the navigators also had the capability for "flex targeting," altering the mission data loads in flight. Flex targeting was used in Operation Iraqi Freedom. Presumably, flex targeting would be done in response to real-time intelligence from offboard sources.

As the transfer alignment continued, the status codes changed from CA to Aligned (AL) after the missiles were fully aligned. When the missile status codes changed from AL to GO, this meant that the missile was aligned, had a mission data load, and GPS keys were loaded. By 1650L, all eight missiles had GO status.

Within 2-30 minutes of launch, the airplane should fly a transfer alignment (TAL) maneuver to provide a wide range of inputs to the CALCM INS to tighten the alignment between it and the OAS. Our TAL involved a left turn to a heading of 210 degrees, followed by straight and level flight for one minute, then a right turn to 290 degrees, followed by straight and level flight for one minute, and then a left turn to return to the launch heading of 250 degrees. To demonstrate the flexibility of the weapon system, the navigators then retargeted missiles No. 1 and No. 2 by swapping their assigned mission data loads.

At 1703L, the crew began the checklist to prepare the missiles for launch. The missiles were prearmed, which changed their arming status on the MFD from SAF (Safe) to RDY (Ready). The pilot unlocked his consent switch. Prearming and the pilot consent switch were safeguards originally designed for the nuclear ALCM. The pilot switched his EVS monitor to repeat the missile launch display on the radar navigator's right MFD. The navigator set the launch mode to manual, which required him to use the guarded launch button on the OAS weapon control panel. Alternatively, he could have set an automated mode in which the OAS initiated the launch. At 1715L, the OAS launch display indicated SAIR. The OAS would have inhibited launch outside of SAIR.

With the bomb doors not able to be opened by OAS due to the fault found during preflight checks, the CALCM exercise was completed by powering down the missiles.

Next, we prepared for attacks with the JDAM. Loading the JDAM SMO software took 10 minutes, so it was 1733L before we could begin to apply power to the 12 (simulated) JDAM guided bombs on our wing pylons. The procedure was similar to the one used for CALCM, with the appropriate changes in OAS weapon control panel buttons being pressed because the weapons were on the wings and not in the bomb bay.

JDAM had no CA mode and no TAL maneuver. When the AL status changed to GO, JDAM was ready to drop. At 1800L, "Chill 25" rolled in on the attack heading for the Belle Fourche, South Dakota, range and contacted the range controller, who cleared us for the simulated attack. The radar navigator entered the coordinates for the center of the target and then specified an attack with a pattern of six JDAMs, two weapons across and three weapons downrange, with a dimension for each side of the rectangle. OAS used the target center coordinates and the pattern information to calculate the individual aimpoint for each JDAM.

While the pilots maintained the attack heading at Flight Level 350 and the navigators prepared the JDAMs for launch, emitters at Belle Fourche began to simulate enemy radars searching for us. At his crew station, the EWO detected and jammed the threats. As the aircraft approached the launch point, the navigator unlocked the weapons using the OAS weapon control panel and the pilot used his consent switch. The OAS indicated time to go to drop and the navigator verbally notified the crew at 1 minute, 20 seconds to go. When the B-52H entered SAIR, the navigator called out: "Crew, standby, 2, 1, JDAM launch, weapons away, turn heading 112," punching off the six bombs with one push of the launch button on the OAS weapon control panel.

At 1821L, we rolled in again for a second pass at the target. The radar navigator demonstrated how he could target a JDAM at an offset to a known point. For example, a ground forward air controller (GFAC) might know his own position through the use of a portable GPS receiver and want to have the B-52 drop a JDAM 500 meters north of his position. The GFAC would radio to the B-52 crew a request. At least three members of the crew would copy the request, because it would be critical to get every element correct to avoid fratricide. The radar navigator would then enter the coordinates into the OAS from the keyboard, specifying an offset 500 meters north of the location of the GFAC. He could also specify the terminal approach heading and impact angle of the JDAM to the target. This could be important if a target were on one side of a steep hill, because the weapon would be ineffective if it tried to fly to the target through the hill. The OAS would calculate if the weapon's kinematics allowed the specified trajectory. If not, the OAS could calculate a trajectory with the approach heading and impact angle being unconstrained.

With the JDAM targeted according to the request of the GFAC, the radar navigator would then radio the GFAC and read back the coordinates from the MFD. If the GFAC verified the targeting, he would clear the B-52 "hot," and then the crew would unlock the weapon. It was this combination of tactics and technology that turned the B-52H into one of the premier close air support platforms in the American arsenal over Afghanistan and Iraq. At 1824L, the navigator salvoed two more JDAMs, and the airplane turned to make a third pass.

During the third pass, the EWO kept the crew informed of the threat environment with a continual running commentary. In response, the pilots performed defensive maneuvers, with 45-degree banked turns in one direction and then another to evade the simulated threats. At the end of the third pass, we turned back toward Minot AFB to give the pilots some practice with instrument approaches. Minot AFB was under a Bird Watch Condition of Moderate, so the regulations did not permit practice approaches in the interests of safety. As we flew in a holding pattern for an hour while waiting for the birds to disperse, I again went downstairs and occupied the seat of the radar navigator to operate the AN/APQ-166 Strategic Radar. The radar was one of the principal navigation sensors, providing position updates to the OAS to correct for INS drift.

The Strategic Radar showed its age, not having the Synthetic Aperture Radar technology of the radars on the B-1B and F-15E that provided an extremely sharp, clear, high-resolution picture of the terrain. A skilled radar navigator could manipulate the tilt of the antenna and the gain of the radar receiver to pick out terrain features. Bodies of water and their shorelines were easy to distinguish. Isolated large buildings, such as hangars, and the runway at Minot AFB were also visible with some skill in radar scope interpretation.

Finally, the birds cleared and we flew four instruments approaches with touch-and-go landings, the last approach ending with a full-stop landing at 2052L. After shutting down and leaving the aircraft, the crew debriefed with maintenance personnel.

Every system and function of the B-52 ultimately serves to put it into position to deliver weapons. The navigator is lifting the protective cover and depressing the launch button on the OAS weapon control panel, releasing a simulated JDAM. (Author)

Combat in the 1990s

High-intensity combat operations against Iraq ended in 1991, but the United States and its coalition partners continued to enforce no-fly zones over northern and southern Iraq (Operation Northern Watch and Operation Southern Watch, respectively). Iraqi air defenses shot at American and British airplanes, which responded to the attacks. On 31 August 1996, Iraqi forces attacked and captured the Kurdish city of Irbil in northern Iraq. Responding to this act, the United States launched Operation Desert Strike.

Three 2nd BW B-52Hs (60-0059, call sign "Duke 01"; 60-0014, call sign "Duke 02"; and 60-0025, call sign "Duke 03") departed Andersen AFB, Guam, on 3 September 1996. Each aircraft was armed with a CSRL and eight AGM-86C CALCMs. The mission commander was Lt. Col. Floyd L. Carpenter, who was the commander of the 96th BS and flew in "Duke 01." "Duke 03" was the spare and returned to base after the other two bombers successfully began their sorties. The other two aircraft proceeded to the Persian Gulf and linked up with F-14 Tomcat escorts from USS *Carl Vinson* (CVN-70).

"Duke 01" launched six missiles and "Duke 02" launched seven missiles (the other missiles malfunctioned and were not launched) at Iraqi air defense sites in the early morning of 4 September 1996 before returning to Guam. The 13,600-mile, 33.9-hour mission required 15 (some sources say 17) tanker sorties and was the combat debut for the B-52H and the CSRL. The aircrews of the aircraft successfully met numerous challenges during the mission. Most of the aerial refuelings required were conducted at night, in stormy tropical weather conditions, with visibility falling to less than a mile. In addition

to the Conventional Air Launched Cruise Missiles (CALCMs), the first wave of attacks in Operation Desert Strike included 14 Tomahawk cruise missiles launched from the USS *Laboon* (DDG-58) and USS *Shiloh* (CG-67). Later, on 4 September 1996, a second wave of 17 Tomahawks from the USS *Russell* (DDG-59), USS *Hewitt* (DD-966), USS *Laboon,* and USS *Jefferson City* (SSN-759) concluded the attacks. For this mission, Lt. Col. Carpenter and the B-52H crews of Operation Desert Strike were awarded the 1996 MacKay Trophy, given for the U.S. Air Force's most meritorious flight of that year.

Although successful in the narrow sense that the targets were hit, Operation Desert Strike had no strategic impact on altering the behavior of Saddam Hussein and his Ba'athist regime in Iraq. On 31 October 1998, the United Nations inspectors verifying Iraqi compliance with the ban on weapons of mass destruction (WMD) were prevented from doing their work, and American forces deployed to the region in Operation Desert Thunder. Included in this deployment were 15 B-52Hs under the command of the 96th Expeditionary Bomb Squadron (EBS), 2nd Air Expeditionary Group (AEG), sent to Diego Garcia, an island in the Indian Ocean previously used as a B-52 base during Operation Desert Storm. The 2nd AEG was first commanded by Col. Wendell L. Griffin and drew its airplanes and personnel from both the 2nd BW at Barksdale AFB and the 5th BW at Minot AFB. On 14 November 1998, a force of B-52Hs was launched toward Iraq. Only 20 minutes from their launch points, Saddam Hussein relented and said that he would allow the inspectors to continue their investigation. The strike was aborted, and

---

B-52H 60-0059 (Operation Desert Strike call sign "Duke 01") was painted with red CALCM symbols after the mission, one for each missile that was launched. (USAF)

B-52H 60-0014 (Operation Desert Strike call sign "Duke 02") also was painted with red CALCM symbols after the mission. (USAF)

the airplanes returned to Diego Garcia. But Saddam Hussein did not keep his word, and Operation Desert Fox was launched on 16 December 1998. The attack on the first night was conducted by carrier aircraft from USS *Enterprise* (CVN-65) and Tomahawk cruise missiles. On the second night, the naval forces were joined by U.S. Air Force and Royal Air Force aircraft based in the Persian Gulf as well as the 2nd AEG.

Fourteen B-52Hs from the 2nd AEG (now commanded by Col. Robert A. Bruley Jr.) launched from Diego Garcia on 17 December 1998. The seven bombers with 2nd BW crews used call signs "Ruben 11" through "Ruben 17." Ruben mission commander Lt. Col. Thomas J. Griffith, the 96th BS commander, flew in "Ruben 11." Seven 5th BW crews used call signs "Blade 21" through "Blade 27," with mission commander Lt. Col. Douglas C. Hayner, the 23rd BS commander, in "Blade 21." All the aircraft were armed with CALCMs on CSRLs. Operation Desert Fox was the combat debut for the CALCM Block 1 variant. The jets refueled from Diego Garcia-based KC-10A tankers on the way to Iraq. After all aircraft successfully refueled, the spare aircraft ("Ruben 15" and "Blade 27") returned to Diego Garcia, and the primary strike aircraft proceeded to their launch points. Several targets were hit, including the al-Tâjî missile manufacturing and repair facility. After launching their missiles, the B-52Hs returned to Diego Garcia, again meeting the KC-10A tankers for refueling over the Indian Ocean. Flight duration for the strike aircraft was approximately 14 hours.

The next day, two B-52Hs using call signs "Blade 21" and "Blade 22" attacked Iraq. After 70 hours, Operation Desert Fox was halted. The 2nd AEG had launched 90 CALCMs. Shortly thereafter, most of the B-52H aircraft and personnel returned to the United States. A few airplanes and crews remained on Diego Garcia to maintain a forward-deployed bomber force in the region.

The 2nd AEG was soon in combat again half a world away, commanded by Col. Floyd L. Carpenter (the Operation Desert Strike airborne mission commander). B-52Hs deployed to RAF Fairford in the United Kingdom in February 1999 in response to the Kosovo crisis. The B-52 flying unit of 2nd AEG was 20th EBS, commanded by Lt. Col. Timothy S. Leaptrott. The other flying units of 2nd AEG were 77th EBS (B-1B) and 22nd Expeditionary Air Refueling Squadron (KC-135R).

With the collapse of diplomatic efforts on 23 March 1999, NATO ordered air strikes against Yugoslav forces. The 20th EBS, 2nd AEG, contributed eight B-52Hs using the call signs "Havoc 11" through "Havoc 18" to the first wave of Operation Allied Force air strikes on 24 March 1999. On that first wave, each B-52H carried eight CALCMs internally, with six aircraft in the primary strike force and two airborne spares. Each primary strike aircraft launched six missiles at targets, primarily air defense systems. In all, 78 AGM-86C and two AGM-142 missiles were launched during Operation Allied Force.

With Yugoslav air defenses largely neutralized, the B-52H attacks then shifted to area bombing against airfields, depots, and units in the field. B-52H strikes on 7 June 1999 against Yugoslav ground forces conducted in concert with Kosovo Liberation Army (KLA) operations were particularly effective. As the Yugoslav forces assembled to combat a KLA offensive, they presented a good target for the B-52Hs, which devastated two battalions. Operation Allied Force combat missions ended on 10 June 1999.

A B-52H from the 96th BS, 2nd BW, piloted by Col. Wendell L. Griffin, 2nd Air Expeditionary Group (AEG) commander, conducts air refueling training near Diego Garcia on 9 December 1998 in preparation for Operation Desert Fox. (Senior Airman Sarah E. Shaw / USAF)

B-52H 60-0033 *Instrument of Destruction* departs RAF Fairford on 23 June 1999 after supporting Operation Allied Force. The markings indicate the aircraft is based at Minot AFB and assigned to 23rd BS, 5th BW. (Staff Sgt. Jim Howard / USAF)

Operation Enduring Freedom

Within hours of the al-Qâ'idah terrorist attacks of 11 September 2001 on the United States, the B-52 force was drawn into events. The VC-25A carrying President George W. Bush (call sign "Air Force One"), departed Florida shortly after the attacks. Several hours later, it landed at Barksdale AFB. Personnel from 2nd BW serviced and secured "Air Force One" while the president made his first public remarks following the attacks. Two hours after landing, the president departed Barksdale AFB. At Minot AFB, Master Sgt. Tina M. Schneider, a supervisor with the 5th Aircraft Maintenance Squadron, 5th BW, poignantly expressed the prevailing attitude of the American military: "We're ready. Give us a call, and let us show what we can do."

Master Sgt. Schneider's wish came true within days. As staff officers assembled the plans to attack al-Qâ'idah terrorists and their Țâlibân hosts in Afghanistan, B-52H and B-1B aircraft, support equipment, and personnel began to move to Diego Garcia to form the 28th Air Expeditionary Wing (AEW). The commander of the 28th AEW was Col. Edward A. Rice Jr. of the 28th BW (the B-1B wing at Ellsworth AFB). The vice commander was Col. Anthony A. Imondi, the vice commander of the 2nd BW. The 28th Expeditionary Mission Support Group, a component of 28th AEW, built Camp

Justice to house the incoming 28th AEW personnel. The 28th AEW's flight operations were handled by the 28th Expeditionary Operations Group (EOG), commanded by Col. Stephen W. Wilson. Within the 28th EOG, B-52H operations were organized into the 20th Expeditionary Bomb Squadron (EBS), commanded by Lt. Col. Paul G. "Taco" Bell, while B-1B operations fell under the 34th EBS, commanded by Lt. Col. Thomas "Bullet" Arko. At first, 28th AEW had eight B-52Hs and eight B-1Bs based on Diego Garcia. The initial complement of aircraft for the 20th EBS arrived at Diego Garcia during 19-22 September 2001 and was composed of 60-0022 (from 96th BS, 2nd BW), 60-0030 (11th BS, 2nd BW), 60-0046 (20th BS, 2nd BW), 60-0049 (11th BS, 2nd BW), 61-0008 (93rd BS, 917th WG), 61-0022 (93rd BS, 917th WG), 61-0023 (20th BS, 2nd BW), and 61-0039 (11th BS, 2nd BW). Also based on Diego Garcia was the 60th AEG, commanded by Col. Darren W. McDew and operating 12 KC-10A tankers.

Operation Enduring Freedom combat began on 7 October 2001. The 28th AEW contribution was six B-52H and six B-1B sorties per day during the first two days, then settling into a sustained rate of four B-52H and four B-1B sorties per day. During the first two weeks of the operation, 28th AEW B-1Bs and B-52Hs based on Diego Garcia,

The ground crew on Diego Garcia prepares B-52H 61-0008 on 2 October 2001 for the upcoming start of Operation Enduring Freedom attacks. The arrowhead marking on the left side of the fuselage indicates this aircraft is permanently assigned to the 93rd BS, 917th WG. (Senior Airman Rebecca M. Luquin / USAF)

Seven B-52Hs line up on the ramp on Diego Garcia. From left, the aircraft are 61-0039 (gold tail band, 11th BS, 2nd BW), 60-0022 (red tail band, 96th BS, 2nd BW), 61-0008 (checkered tail band, 93rd BS, 917th WG), and four others. To the right of the B-52Hs are the KC-10As of 60th AEG. (Senior Airman Rebecca M. Luquin / USAF)

509th BW B-2As flying to Afghanistan nonstop from their base in Missouri, carrier-based aircraft from the USS *Enterprise* (CVN-65) and USS *Carl Vinson* (CVN-70), and BGM-109 Tomahawk cruise missiles fired from ships attacked fixed targets in Afghanistan. For the first time, the B-52H dropped the GBU-31 JDAM and CBU-103 WCMD in combat.

Capt. Bryan "Squarebush" Roundtree, a B-52H radar navigator, described the highlights of his first combat mission over Afghanistan. On 9 October 2001, his crew launched from Diego Garcia in B-52H 61-0022 as part of a two-ship formation on an on-call close air support (XCAS) mission, armed with 12 GBU-31(V)1 JDAMs and 27 Mk 82 bombs. Over Afghanistan, the flight split up, and Roundtree's crew began receiving targets over voice SATCOM. First, the B-52H hit a terrorist camp near Kandahâr with five JDAMs. Next, it flew north to deliver one JDAM on a radar installation west of Mazâr-i-Sharîf, followed by dropping six JDAMs on a terrorist camp near Mazâr-i-Sharîf. Then the B-52H returned to Kandahâr to deliver 27 Mk 82 bombs on the terrorist camp to complete its destruction. After completing its "grand tour of Afghanistan," 61-0022 returned to Diego Garcia, having logged 13 hours of flight time.

Two additional B-52H bombers arrived in late October. With these reinforcements, the 28th AEW's workload increased to 10 bomber sorties each day.

Starting on 21 October 2001, the focus of the air offensive shifted from planned attacks on fixed targets to the XCAS mission in close cooperation with special operations forces. With no American conventional ground forces yet in Afghanistan, American special operations teams from the CIA and the U.S. Army's 5th Special Forces Group (Airborne) linked up with anti-Tâlibân fighters of the Northern Alliance. The Northern Alliance fighters flushed out the Tâlibân and al-Qâ'idah from their hiding spots in Afghanistan's forbidding terrain. Then U.S. Air Force forward air controllers attached to the special operations teams used their GPS units and laser rangefinders to precisely determine the geographic coordinates of the enemy and called in strikes with AN/PRC-117F multiband digital radios.

The bombers departed Diego Garcia for the five-hour flight to Afghanistan with no planned targets and refueled from tankers before entering Afghanistan. Over Afghanistan, they orbited until given a target by the CAOC located at Prince Sulţân Air Base, Saudi Arabia. Satellite communications connected the CAOC with the special operations teams and the airborne bombers. In the target area, the bombers' crews communicated directly with the air controllers on the ground to coordinate the delivery of weapons. Thus, the B-52H aircrews used the modernizations of the previous decade (smart weapons and their SMOs, GPS, AN/ARC-210, and satellite communications) to devastate an enemy unlike the adversary for which the B-52 had been conceived more than 50 years earlier. After five to 10 hours over Afghanistan, the B-52H flew the five-hour return flight to Diego Garcia.

The combination of American special operations forces, indigenous troops, and airpower was decisive. One key mission was flown on 5 November 2001 in B-52H 60-0022, with the call sign "Sinai 01." The 93rd BS crew was aircraft commander Lt. Col. Keith D. Schultz, co-pilot Maj. Jeff Woods, radar navigator Lt. Col. Tim Mers, navigator

B-52H 61-0022, loaded with JDAMs, waits at Diego Garcia for the initiation of Operation Enduring Freedom combat operations. (Senior Airman Rebecca M. Luquin / USAF)

Leaders of the 28th AEW pose with munitions troops. Col. Rice is in the front row, third from left, and Col. Imondi is at right in the front row. The Mk 84 bomb bodies are packed four to a pallet. Depending on the kits attached to the body, the bomb body can be configured as an unguided bomb, a laser-guided bomb, or a JDAM. In the background is the motor vessel (MV) *Maj. Bernard F. Fisher* (T-AK 4396), a cargo ship dedicated to transporting Air Force munitions. She is named after a U.S. Air Force officer decorated with the Medal of Honor in the Vietnam War. (Senior Airman Rebecca M. Luquin / USAF)

B-52H 61-0022, of the 93rd BS, 917th WG, taxis to the runway for departure from Diego Garcia on 7 October 2001 as part of the first wave of attacks on Afghanistan. Personnel with the 28th AEW lined the sides of the taxiway to cheer on the aircrews. (Senior Airman Rebecca M. Luquin / USAF)

By 10 October 2001, B-52H 61-0008 sported crude but heartfelt nose art memorializing the losses suffered by the New York City Fire Department as a result of the 11 September 2001 terrorist attacks by al-Qâ'idah. The "FDNY" is dull red, and the rest of the nose art is black. Four small black tomahawk symbols under the 917th WG shield are combat mission markings. (Senior Airman Rebecca M. Luquin / USAF)

Maj. Christopher Talbot, and EWO Maj. Mark Alvarez. The following account was taken nearly verbatim from 28th AEW internal documentation.

After departure from Diego Garcia and over Afghanistan, "Sinai 01" received an emergency tasking from the Central Command CAOC to support Operation Detachment Alpha (ODA) 595, 5th Special Forces Group (Airborne) (call signs "Tiger 02A" and "Tiger 02C"), which were being overrun by Țâlibân forces south of Mazâr-i-Sharîf, Afghanistan. "Sinai 01" flew to the far northern portion of Afghanistan at maximum speed and made contact with "Tiger 02C." On initial contact, a number of difficulties became apparent. "Sinai 01" made three passes delivering two GBU-31(V)1 JDAMs against the attacking Țâlibân forces but was ineffective since "Tiger 02C" derived the coordinates from an inaccurate Escape and Evasion chart. Due to mountainous terrain and ground radio limitations, "Sinai 01" had to orbit directly over the position of "Tiger 02C" to maintain communication. Even then, ground transmissions were garbled and barely readable, requiring multiple transmissions to complete a targeting message. Due to ground radio limitations, "Sinai 01" had to relay communications between the elements of "Tiger 02," an E-3 AWACS, and the CAOC, vastly increasing the workload since each transmission required reconfiguring the aircraft radio setup (due to a single encryption device) for each party. Target coordinates were passed via voice transmission, copied and cross-checked by the entire crew. To deliver weapons, "Sinai 01" had to proceed 30 miles outbound, and then turn 180 degrees to reach the JDAM launch window. With "Sinai 01" at "bingo" fuel level (minimum fuel to return to base) and no additional strike assets available in country, Lt. Col. Schultz coordinated an emergency aerial refueling to extend their time on station. The refueling rendezvous was northeast of Mazâr-i-Sharîf, taking "Sinai 01" well below the minimum fuel required to reach home station. Lt. Col. Schultz coordinated a viable divert plan, allowing "Sinai 01" to continue with the emergency refueling over northern Afghanistan despite being within the altitude range of enemy anti-aircraft systems. Lt. Col. Schultz completed a nonstandard rejoin and expeditiously took 60,000 pounds of fuel while battling nearly complete obscuration due to the setting sun and extended their combat presence by three hours. "Sinai 01" returned to the battlefield. "Tiger 02C" had been forced to retreat into the mountains just ahead of advancing Țâlibân forces. Since "Tiger 02C" had recorded the GPS coordinates of his overrun position, he was able to pass three sets of target coordinates. "Sinai 01" released direct hits on the forward observation post and two nearby targets of troops and equipment.

With the threat in the north removed, "Sinai 01" then coordinated with "Tiger 02A" in the west to facilitate one of the most technologically innovative attacks of the war. The local Northern Alliance leader believed he had located the senior Țâlibân commander in a bunker near the village of Chârsû, where the main attack was taking place. Unfortunately, the bunker was located on the high point of a ridge. Anything less than precise location of the target could mean the impact of a JDAM in the village itself, creating unacceptable collateral damage. Evasion charts had already proven inaccurate, and ground laser targeting devices were not available. Fortunately, an RQ-1 Predator unmanned aerial vehicle in the area provided visual imagery to the CAOC and supporting Joint Intelligence Center (JIC) thousands of miles away in Saudi Arabia. In the JIC, intelligence specialists quickly mensurated the target and passed exact target information back to "Tiger 02A" on the ground and "Sinai 01" overhead. "Sinai 01" delivered a single JDAM at 1800, scoring a direct hit on the bunker, eliminating the last symbol of local Ṭâlibân control. Northern Alliance horsemen then overran the bunker and quickly occupied Chârsû, driving the last remnants of Ṭâlibân troops from the area. With the Ṭâlibân command in disarray, "Tiger 02A" called for a last strike against the enemy cavalry regiment massing for an offensive charge. "Sinai 01" released 27 Mk 82s into the heart of the advancing forces. The swath of destruction opened a gap for the Northern Alliance that would never be regained by the Ṭâlibân.

While it was not known at the time, this was the key battle in the fight for Mazâr-i-Sharîf. "Sinai 01" returned to Diego Garcia, having logged 16.6 hours on the sortie, one of the longest B-52H sorties of Operation Enduring Freedom. Allied Afghan forces with their American special operations advisors attacked through the gap blasted in the enemy, capturing Mazâr-i-Sharîf on 9 November 2001. The fall of Mazâr-i-Sharîf triggered the collapse of Ṭâlibân positions throughout northern Afghanistan.

B-52H attacks on 12 November 2001 in support of the 5th Special Forces Group (Airborne) shattered the Ṭâlibân forces around Kabul, the Afghan capital. Kabul fell on 13 November 2001.

The war continued after Kabul fell. During the evening of 1 December 2001, another 93rd BS crew assigned to 20th EBS with the call sign "Helens 54" departed from Diego Garcia. The crew of "Helens 54" consisted of aircraft commander Lt. Col. Scott Forrest, co-pilot Maj. Sam Holmes, radar navigator Maj. Joseph Jones, navigator Maj. Bruce Gootee, and EWO Maj. Chris Rounds. The B-52H was armed with 16 CBU-103 WCMDs on HSABs and 27 Mk 82 bombs in the bay. As usual, the B-52H refueled over the water and then crossed over Pakistan into Afghanistan. By now, the main fighting had moved south, and the B-52H orbited southwest of Kandahâr on an XCAS mission. Following a request received over voice SATCOM to provide support for special operations forces and their Afghan allies who were advancing up highway M4 to Kandahâr, "Helens 54" turned toward the target area. In the target area, "Helens 54" worked with a controller on the ground and an airborne forward air controller (call sign "Blue Ridge"). F-14 Tomcats (call sign "Ebert") were already in the area, attacking the enemy in fortified positions with laser-guided bombs. Ebert flight was attacked by shoulder-launched missiles, and the controller requested that "Helens 54" suppress the missile fire. From an altitude of 38,000 feet, safely above the ceiling of the missiles, "Helens 54" made five passes, dropping five Mk 82 bombs on the first four passes and seven on the last pass. The controller reported "shacks" as the highly accurate bombs hit their targets.

By 1 December 2001, 20th EBS had logged 375 sorties. The 28th AEW plus the few 509th BW missions had made up only 10 percent of the strike missions over Afghanistan but delivered 65 percent of the total air-dropped weapons, including two AGM-142 Have Nap missiles.

Tragedy struck on 5 December 2001, when a B-52H was involved in fratricide. ODA 574, 5th Special Forces Group (Airborne), commanded by Capt. Jason Amerine, was approaching Kandahâr. The forward air controller assigned to ODA 574 had just

Col. Imondi, vice commander of the 28th AEW, poses in front of B-52H 61-0022 of the 93rd BS, 917th WG. The aircraft's nose art memorializes the New York Police Department officers killed in the 11 September 2001 attacks. The "NYPD" is white, and the rest of the nose art is black. When this photograph was taken on 14 November 2001, the aircraft had 16 tomahawk mission markings. (Senior Airman Rebecca M. Luquin / USAF)

Munitions troops use an MHU-83C/E loader to load a GBU-31(V)1 JDAM with a DSU-33B/B radar proximity fuze on B-52H 61-0032 of the 93rd BS, 917th WG. (Staff Sgt. Shane Cuomo / USAF)

finished calling in an airstrike from an F/A-18 Hornet when the battery powering his GPS receiver expired. He changed the battery, and after the GPS powered up, he radioed the coordinates on its display to the B-52. The forward air controller did not realize that when the GPS powered up, the coordinates that it initially displayed were not those of the target that it had previously calculated, but the coordinates of the GPS receiver itself. Therefore the B-52 delivered the JDAM onto ODA 574, killing Master Sgt. Jefferson D. Davis, Sgt. 1st Class David H. Petithory, Staff Sgt. Brian C. Prosser, and several friendly Afghan fighters. Many friendly personnel were also wounded.

As the remnants of the Ţâlibân and al-Qâʿidah melted into the mountains of Afghanistan, bombers continued to fly XCAS missions, although they often returned to base without having delivered any weapons. In December 2001, the 28th AEW B-1Bs transferred to 405th AEW, based at Thumrait Air Base, Oman. On 4 February 2002, the unit on Diego Garcia was redesignated as the 40th AEW. The B-52 flying squadron of the 40th AEW was redesignated the 40th EBS.

During 2-16 March 2002, the fighting in Afghanistan entered a new phase with the launch of Operation Anaconda against al-Qâʿidah forces in the rugged Shâh-i-Kôt region near the border with Pakistan. Operation Anaconda was the first major American offensive primarily conducted by conventional infantry rather than special operations forces and

Aircraft and personnel were rotated through Diego Garcia and then back home. The initial B-52 resources were drawn primarily from Barksdale AFB, but by 22 February 2002, B-52H 60-0015 *Antidote* of the 23rd BS, 5th BW, was engaged in operations. (Senior Airman Rebecca M. Luquin / USAF)

Whereas the 917th WG used tomahawks as mission markings, 2nd BW used scimitars. B-52H 61-0016 *Free Bird* also has 15 CALCM silhouettes. Since the CALCM was not used during Operation Enduring Freedom, these must have been retained from earlier operations. (Senior Airman Rebecca M. Luquin / USAF)

local allies. The objective of the attack was to trap and destroy the enemy. Because of the extremely rough terrain, the American force had no artillery, and all of its fire support was provided by aircraft. B-52Hs from the 40th EBS were heavily involved in the fighting, flying an average of five sorties per day during the operation. Some B-52H close air support strikes were highly effective. Three reconnaissance teams from the secretive Joint Special Operations Command (JSOC) with the call signs "India," "Juliet," and "Mako 31" established observations posts in commanding terrain overlooking the Shâh-i-Kôt, from which they directed attacks by B-52Hs and other aircraft. In one action on 2 March, "Juliet" observed six al-Qâʻidah fighters setting up an ambush against the 2nd Battalion, 187th Infantry Regiment. The team contacted a B-52H, and several minutes later a rectangular pattern of six JDAMs hit the enemy, killing four and wounding one. However, Operation Anaconda was rife with command and control problems. JSOC and the conventional Army units did not have unity of command, resulting in confusion and conflict. Furthermore, air commanders were not brought in on the planning of the operation. In one case, poor coordination caused a B-52H to return to Diego Garcia with a full load of bombs despite the raging battle below. One of the most harrowing incidents of the battle occurred when a B-52H almost dropped a salvo of bombs directly into the flight path of an AC-130 gunship flying below it.

While the B-52H aircrews were the tip of the spear in Operation Enduring Freedom, equally important work was being done by the maintenance and logistics personnel of the 28th Expeditionary Maintenance Group. Working daily 12-hour shifts, seven days a week, the maintainers turned aircraft between missions to meet mission

This 40th EBS pilot is wearing a tan flight suit. He has sanitized his uniform by removing the patch that was fastened to his right shoulder with Velcro. The Combat Track II computer in its folded position is visible in the upper right on the photograph, and the American flag on the flare shield is for the benefit of the photographer. (Tech. Sgt. Richard Freeland / USAF)

A 40th AEG B-52H refuels from a KC-135 over the Indian Ocean on a 13 March 2006 mission to Afghanistan. B-52 support of Operation Enduring Freedom would not have been possible without aerial refueling, which is the most challenging maneuver for B-52 pilots. (Staff Sgt. Doug Nicodemus / USAF)

A B-52H with the 40th AEG is undergoing a phase inspection at Andersen AFB in Guam. The spoilers on top of the wings, used for roll control and as airbrakes, are in the open position on this aircraft. (Master Sgt. Val Gempis / USAF)

A B-52H carrying the markings of the 96th BS, 2nd BW departs Diego Garcia for a bomb run over Afghanistan. As the long, flexible wing develops lift during the takeoff run, its bends up and the outrigger landing gear no longer touch the ground. (Senior Airman Rebecca M. Luquin / USAF)

B-52H 60-003 has "God Bless America" written on the nose, and the emblems of the New York Police Department and the Fire Department of New York beneath "God Bless America." The tomahawk mission markings are indicative of a B-52H deployed from the 917th WG. (Senior Airman Rebecca M. Luquin / USAF)

requirements. On the return flight to Diego Garcia, the aircrew would radio in problems so technicians and spare parts could be readied. The command post staff and the air traffic played important roles in bringing the B-52Hs back to Diego Garcia.

If the aircraft landed with any hung weapons, first it was taxied to an isolated area and the hung weapons were safed. After engine shut-down in a parking spot on the Diego Garcia ramp, the aircrew departed for their debriefing while the crew chiefs chocked the airplane. Security forces set up a security perimeter around the B-52H and an entry control point. While the crew chiefs and fuel specialists refueled the B-52H, the weapons loaders moved the weapons into position, and the supply specialists issued any parts needed for repairs to the mechanics and technicians. After refueling was completed, the weapons were loaded and repairs made. The crew chiefs serviced the aircraft with nitrogen, liquid oxygen, hydraulic fluid, and engine oil. Aerospace ground equipment technicians serviced the extensive range of ground support equipment needed to maintain and operate the B-52H.

Keeping the aged B-52Hs airworthy posed special challenges. When an inspection revealed the fraying of a control cable for spoilers, the entire B-52H fleet was grounded for one day in 2002 until all the aircraft were inspected and cleared. Two aerial refuelings per sortie put considerable wear and tear on the aerial refueling equipment of the B-52H.

While the aircraft were readied for the next mission, the staff of Lt. Col. Jim "Bucky" Butts, 28th Expeditionary Operations Support Squadron, was also busy. Intelligence and mission planning personnel assembled mission folders and loaded data into the OAS Data Transfer Unit Cartridges. Meteorologists prepared forecasts. Life support technicians cleaned, repaired, and tested aircrew equipment such as helmets and oxygen masks. Aircrews usually flew a mission every three days, with the time between missions used for rest, squadron duties, and planning and briefing their next mission.

The intensive support effort extended far beyond Diego Garcia. Every 300 flight hours, a B-52H had to undergo a phase inspection, for which Diego Garcia was neither equipped nor staffed. At first, the aircraft were flown 20 hours back to the continental United States for this work. To minimize the number of aircraft in the phase inspection pipeline, the 40th AEW set up a phase inspection line "only" 11 flight hours away at Andersen AFB in Guam. During phase inspection, the B-52Hs underwent three days of inspections, followed by repairs that often took a week or more, and, finally, a functional check flight before their return to combat.

Logistics was a major challenge, with Diego Garcia being at the end of a very long supply line. In particular, the missions consumed JDAMs at a high rate (approximately 150 per day), requiring replenishment by airlift. The fuel troops pumped 1.1 million gallons of JP-8 jet fuel per day. Even parking aircraft presented a problem, with bombers, tankers, airlifters, and other aircraft jostling for ramp space on the small island.

The 40th AEW downsized in 2003 after the completion of the major combat phase of Operation Iraqi Freedom and was redesignated the 40th AEG. Although smaller than before, it continued to conduct active combat operations over Afghanistan. Through April 2006, B-52H bombers were deployed to the 40th AEG on Diego Garcia, flying daily missions over Afghanistan before being relieved in May 2006 by B-1Bs.

During a visit to Diego Garcia, Brigadier General Curtis M. Bedke, the 2nd BW commander (center) flanked by two maintenance officers stand in front of an AGM-142 Have Nap missile. (Senior Airman Rebecca M. Luquin / USAF)

A munitions maintainer fits a B-11 bomb shackle to the Mk 82 bomb. The shackle attaches the bomb to the rack in the bomb bay and releases the bomb on command. The bomb has a MAU-93/B conical low-drag conical fin set for high-altitude delivery. (Senior Airman Rebecca M. Luquin / USAF)

Colonel Imondi carries on the US Air Force tradition of sending greeting to the enemy. The munition is a GBU-31(V)1/B JDAM. The nose plug on the bomb covered an FMU-139A/B fuze that detonated the bomb on impact or after a ground-programmed delay. (Senior Airman Rebecca M. Luquin / USAF)

A load crew uses an MJ-1 lift truck to load a Mk 82 bomb into the bomb bay of a B-52H on Diego Garcia. Each Mk 82 bomb with MAU-93/B finds weighed 532 pounds including 192 pounds of high explosive filler. (Senior Airman Rebecca M. Luquin / USAF)

Operation Iraqi Freedom

Operation Iraqi Freedom followed Operation Enduring Freedom, with the objective of toppling the Ba'athist regime of Saddam Hussein that ruled Iraq.

In preparation for Operation Iraqi Freedom, the 40th AEW on Diego Garcia was reinforced with additional B-52H bombers, for a total of 14. The 40th AEW primarily drew its aircraft and personnel from Barksdale AFB. Col. Floyd L. Carpenter commanded the 40th AEW. Under Carpenter were Col. George R. Gagnon's 40th Expeditionary Operations Group and Col. Karen S. Wilhelm's 40th Expeditionary Maintenance Group. The B-52H flying unit of the 40th AEW was the 40th EBS, commanded by Lt. Col. Timothy M. Ray. Additional B-52Hs from Barksdale AFB were assigned to 7th AEW, based at Andersen AFB in Guam and commanded by Col. Jonathan D. George. The B-1Bs and B-52Hs of the 7th AEW struck Iraq and deterred North Korea and China while the United States was preoccupied with Operation Iraqi Freedom.

U.S. Air Force Europe activated a B-52H unit for Operation Iraqi Freedom, the 457th AEG based at RAF Fairford in the United Kingdom. The 457th AEG was commanded by Col. Daniel J. Charchian, assigned to the unit from his normal duties as the commander of the 5th Operations Group, 5th BW, at Minot AFB. It was primarily staffed with Minot personnel. The strike force of 457th AEG was composed of the 23rd EBS formed around the core of 23rd BS from Minot's 5th BW with 14 B-52Hs commanded by Lt. Col.

Robert F. Bussian. The 457th AEG carried the lineage and battle honors of the 457th Bombardment Group (Heavy) of World War II fame.

Air patrols over northern and southern Iraq (Operations Northern Watch and Southern Watch, respectively) had been nearly continuous since Operation Desert Storm in 1991, and numerous exchanges of fire between American and allied aircraft and Iraqi air defense forces had degraded the latter. In the run-up to Operation Iraqi Freedom, the intensity of attacks on the air defenses increased so that when Operation Iraqi Freedom formally began on 19 March 2003, the American led coalition already had achieved air supremacy over Iraq. The first priority for B-52 attacks, which began on 21 March 2003, was a series of strategic attacks against command, control, and communications targets. The objective of the "Shock and Awe" campaign was to paralyze and decapitate the regime. At Diego Garcia, 10 B-52Hs launched for the first wave of attacks, including the first aircraft to carry JDAM and CALCM on the same sortie, and the first combat uses of the AGM-86C CALCM Block 1A and AGM-86D CALCM Block 2. Eight B-52Hs launched from Fairford in the first wave of attacks. Master Sgt. Tina M. Schneider, so eager to strike back after the 11 September 2001 attacks, was the night shift flight line superintendent at Fairford and made sure the bombers were ready to go. When the lead jet from Fairford, flown by Lt. Col. Bussian, aborted because of an avionics problem, the lead position was

The ground crew is using an A/S32R-11 fuel servicing tank truck to fill a 23rd EBS, 457th AEG, B-52H at RAF Fairford in preparation for a mission over Iraq. The A/S32R-11 carries 6,000 gallons of fuel and pumps it at 600 gallons per minute. (Airman 1st Class Stacia M. Willis / USAF)

Senior Airman Benjamin Davis, assigned to the 5th Expeditionary Maintenance Squadron, 457th AEG, marshals B-52H 60-0060 *Iron Butterfly* out of its parking spot on 21 March 2003, the first day of B-52H combat missions in Operation Iraqi Freedom. (Tech. Sgt. Jason Tudor / USAF)

taken by B-52H 60-0060 *Iron Butterfly*, commanded by Capt. Jason D. Horton.

The effectiveness of the "Shock and Awe" campaign was unclear. Although it did not bring down the regime, it degraded the regime's ability to control its military, and may have contributed to paralysis and demoralization, and thereby assisted the rapid advance of American and British ground forces. A total of 153 CALCMs were expended during the campaign: 75 by the 40th EBS, 40th AEW, and 78 by the 23rd EBS, 457th AEG.

The "Shock and Awe" phase of the B-52 participation in Operation Iraqi Freedom was followed by interdiction and close air support sorties that were closely coordinated with the ground forces. As in Afghanistan, the previous decade's investment in avionics and precision-guided weapons combined with the long range and heavy payload of the B-52H made it a fearsome weapon system. The 40th AEW supported the U.S. Army's V Corps and I Marine Expeditionary Force (I MEF), advancing into Iraq from Kuwait. The 457th AEG worked with the Carrier Air Wing 3 (CVW-3), based on USS *Harry S. Truman* (CVN-75) and CVW-8, based on the USS *Theodore Roosevelt* (CVN-71), to support the American, Australian, and British special operations forces and their Kurdish Peshmerga allies in northern Iraq.

The flight of "Dogwood 30" illustrated the great robustness of the B-52 and the skills of its crews. On 30 March 2003, a highly experienced crew consisting of Maj. William Winans, Maj. Greg Anderson, Maj. Charles Bailey, Maj. Pat McGlade, and Maj. Lane Humphreys launched from Diego Garcia in B-52H 60-0015, carrying a load of 12 GBU-31(V)1 JDAMs and 27 Mk 82 bombs. Inbound to Iraq and after the first aerial refueling, the No. 7 engine failed. Although the aircraft was heavily loaded, the crew decided to press on to the target in spite of its reduced performance. When it was 100 kilometers south of Baghdad, heavy but ineffective anti-aircraft fire began to be directed at "Dogwood 30," and the crew learned that their planned air defense suppression package of F-16C and EA-6B aircraft was cancelled. Now relying on its own defensive avionics, "Dogwood 30" continued on alone to penetrate the Baghdad "Super MEZ" (Missile Engagement Zone). During the run-in to the target, several missiles were fired at "Dogwood 30," although none was guided. The crew released a pattern of 12 JDAMs on positions of the al-Madînah Division of the Iraqi Republican Guard. Departing the target area, two more missiles flew toward "Dogwood 30." The electronic warfare officer identified guidance signals from an SA-3 surface-to-air missile system, and the pilots broke left in an evasive maneuver and dived 2,000 feet. Between 15 and 20 seconds after leaving the threat ring, the crew felt a huge bump. It felt like an explosion, but there was no damage, and the cause remains a mystery. Next "Dogwood 30" was assigned an ammunition storage area as a target and circled around to penetrate the Baghdad "Super MEZ" again. After dropping the Mk 82 load on the target, "Dogwood 30" departed Iraq. Before the aerial refueling on the return trip, No. 8 engine failed. The crew met the challenge of an aerial refueling at night and in poor weather, with two engines out on one side. After declaring an emergency, the actual landing at Diego Garcia was uneventful, and the crew concluded their 16-hour mission.

Operation Iraqi Freedom was the combat debut for the CBU-105 SFW. B-52H 60-0007 (call sign "Throw 35") and its crew of aircraft commander Lt. Col. Stockton, co-pilot 1st Lt. Crooks, radar navigator Capt. Sarah L. Hall, navigator 1st Lt. Berne, and

A B-52H bound for Iraq roars down the runway at RAF Fairford on 7 April 2003. The highly flexible wings are already lifting, and the outrigger landing gears are no longer in contact with the ground. (Airman 1st Class Stacia M. Willis / USAF)

B-52H 60-0023, the flagship of the 23rd BS, 5th BW, launches on the 457th AEG's 100th Operation Iraqi Freedom B-52 combat sortie on 10 April 2003. (Airman 1st Class Stacia M. Willis / USAF)

electronic warfare officer Capt. Kim launched from Diego Garcia on 1 April 2003, armed with 16 CBU-105B/B weapons and 27 Mk 82 bombs. After the inbound leg of the flight and two aerial refuelings, "Throw 35" contacted a I MEF forward air controller on the ground, who gave the coordinates for an Iraqi ammunition dump that he wanted destroyed. The OAS then lost its navigation solution, requiring Hall and Berne to realign it with radar position fixes. Fifteen minutes after the initial contact with the forward air controller, "Throw 35" delivered all its Mk 82 bombs on the ammunitions dump. In the words of the controller, the bombs "laid waste" to the target.

Next, a I MEF forward controller requested that "Throw 35" attack a column of Iraqi armored vehicles. Capt. Hall selected two CBU-105B/B weapons for the attack. At the computed release point, the weapons dropped. Guided by their WCMD tail kits, the weapons descended, opening up at the set altitude to each release 10 BLU-108B/B munitions, which in turn each deployed four submunitions. The 80 submunitions descended by parachute, searching for targets with their infrared sensors. Upon detecting targets, the submunitions fired explosively formed projectiles into the thin top armor of the Iraqi vehicles. Half of the column was destroyed, and survivors surrendered to the Marines. Interestingly, U.S. Marine Corps sources consulted by the author have no record of this attack.

"Throw 35" was still carrying 14 CBU-105B/B weapons and was ready to use them.

Technicians install a Litening II pod in preparation for its first use in combat on the B-52H. (Airman 1st Class Stacia M. Willis / USAF)

Crewmembers of B-52H 61-0021 are seen after the "Facet 32" mission of 11 April 2003, when they made the first combat drop of a laser-guided bomb from a B-52. From left are co-pilot Lt. Col. Rob Hyde, aircraft commander Lt. Col. Keith Schultz, radar navigator Lt. Col. William Floyd, navigator Capt. Patrick McDonald, and electronic warfare officer Maj. Trey Moriss. (Master Sgt. Andrew Lynch / USAF)

B-52H 61-0008 takes off from RAF Fairford on 7 April 2003. This aircraft was deployed to the 457th AEG from the 93rd BS, 917th WG, and wears that unit's markings, including the distinctive Indian head on the tip tanks. When deployed to an AEG or AEW, all differences between regular and AFRC personnel equipment and personnel disappeared. Although marked as an AFRC aircraft, this particular sortie may well have been flown by an active duty crew. (Airman 1st Class Stacia M. Willis / USAF)

An E-8C Joint Surveillance Target Attack Radar System (JSTARS) aircraft gave "Throw 35" coordinates for massed armored vehicles in the Baghdad area. The B-52H dropped four more weapons and then returned to Diego Garcia, landing after more than 16 hours of flying.

For Operation Iraqi Freedom, B-52H 61-0021, with its Litening II pod and specially trained Reserve crew from the 93rd BS, was assigned to the 457th AEG. On 11 April 2003, B-52H 61-0021, with three GBU-12D/B Paveway II laser-guided bombs in the bay, 16 CBU-103 cluster bombs under the wings, a Litening II targeting pod, and the call sign "Facet 32," took off from RAF Fairford for Iraq. The crew consisted of aircraft commander Lt. Col. Keith Schultz, co-pilot Lt. Col. Rob Hyde, radar navigator Lt. Col. William Floyd, navigator Capt. Patrick McDonald, and EWO Maj. Trey Moriss. Once over Iraq, "Facet 32" used the targeting pod to search for enemy forces in the area between Mosul and the Syrian border. Then the crew proceeded to Al Sahra airfield northwest of Tikrît, Iraq, penetrating an MEZ defended by SA-2 and SA-8 surface-to-air missile systems. Lt. Col. Floyd acquired and designated a command center at Al Sahra with the Litening II pod, and Capt. McDonald released a single GBU-12D/B that destroyed it. Lt. Col. Schultz then maneuvered "Facet 32" around for attacks on more targets with the two remaining GBU-12D/B bombs, followed by attacks with the cluster bombs.

Major combat operations in Iraq were declared to be over on 1 May 2003. By that date, 280 B-52H sorties had been flown for Operation Iraqi Freedom, with only a handful coming later.

Capt. Michelle Gillespie, a 40th EBS navigator, checks conditions over a target during a mission to Iraq. At her left is a laptop computer that is part of the Combat Track II system. (Tech. Sgt. Richard Freeland / USAF)

During OIF, Andersen AFB on Guam hosted the 7th AEW with its B-52H and B-1B bombers. B-52H 60-0010 has an "LA" tail code and a blue tail band, signifying that it was deployed from the 20th BS, 2nd BW, at Barksdale AFB. (Staff Sgt. Charlene M. Franken / USAF)

B-52H 60-0003 of the 40th EBS, 40th AEW has a full load of post-9/11 regalia, including New York police and fire department markings under the "God Bless America" art and a Bossier City police logo after the "God Bless America" art. (Tech. Sgt. Richard Freeland / USAF)

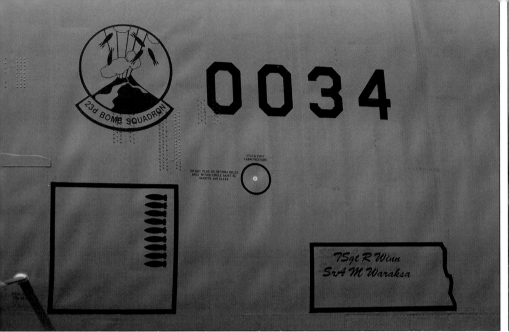

B-52H 60-0034 retained OIF mission markings a year after returning to Minot AFB from RAF Fairford. The 23rd BS logo is above the mission markings and forward of the "0051." All markings are black. (Author)

B-52H 60-0033, a 23rd BS, 5th BW aircraft deployed to the 457th AEG, returns with empty bomb racks from an OIF sortie on 21 March 2003. This is the same aircraft in the photograph on page 61. (Master Sgt. Andrew E. Lynch / USAF)

Whereas B-52H 60-0034 only dropped bombs, B-52H 60-0047 had mission markings that indicated that it delivered both bombs and CALCMs. The outline of North Dakota, which normally contains the names of the crew chiefs, is empty. (Author)

Maintenance is a never-ending task. Airmen of the 457th AEG are giving this B-52H a wash to prevent corrosion. It takes about six hours to wash one bomber, and each bomber receives a wash every 120 days. (Airman 1st Class Stacia M. Willis / USAF)

B-52H 60-0028, with the 96th BS, 2nd BW, at Barksdale AFB in 2005 carried the markings of the 8th Air Force flagship.

B-52H 60-0031 was with the 49th Test and Evaluation Squadron, 53rd WG, at Barksdale AFB in 2004.

B-52H 60-0036 was with the 419th Flight Test Squadron, 412th Test Wing, at Edwards AFB in 2004.

B-52H 61-0036 was with the 325th BS, 92nd BW, at Fairchild AFB in 1994.

B-52H 61-0029 was with the 93rd BS, 917th WG, at Barksdale AFB in 2005. Until 1997, Air Force Reserve aircraft were marked with "AFRES" on their tails. When the Air Force Reserve was redesignated the Air Force Reserve Comand in 1997, the marking changed to "AFRC."

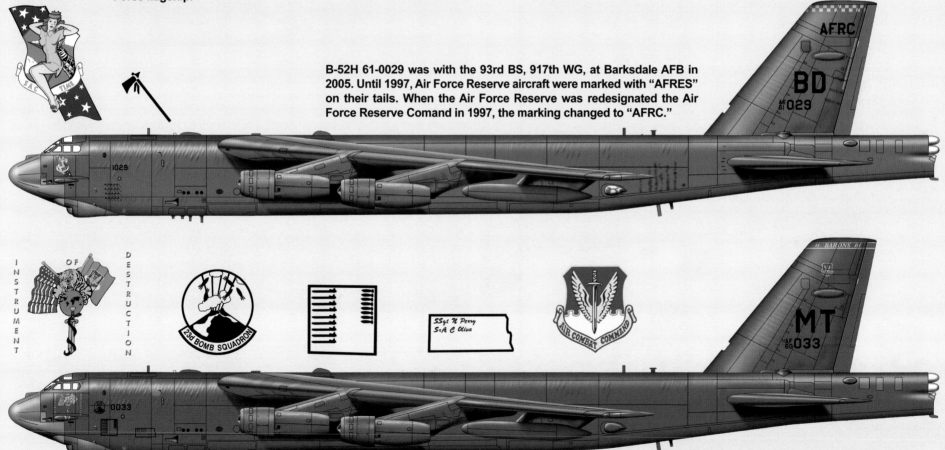

B-52H 60-0033 was with the 23rd BS, 5th BW, at Minot AFB in 2004. The aircraft retained its mission markings from Operation Iraqi Freedom.

NASA B-52H

Two B-52s were modified as motherships for the X-15 research program, NB-52A 52-003 ("Balls Three") and NB-52B 52-008 ("Balls Eight"). NB-52A 52-003 was retired in 1969. "Balls Eight" remained in service, its last mission being the launch of the third X-43A Hyper-X scramjet-powered hypersonic aircraft on 16 November 2004, which set an absolute speed record of Mach 9.6 for aircraft with air-breathing propulsion. On 17 December 2004, "Balls Eight" was formally retired. At its retirement, it was by far the oldest B-52 remaining and paradoxically the one with the least flight hours. But as the only remaining early model B-52, it was an orphan and logistically unsupportable due to a lack of spare parts.

NASA and the USAF desired a replacement for NB-52B. With the retirement of the last B-52G in 1995, the only remaining B-52 model in service was the B-52H. NASA had considered using one of the B-52G aircraft no longer used by the USAF, but wanted to avoid repeating the problems associated with maintaining an orphan, and so decided to use a B-52H. The USAF loaned B-52H 61-0025 to NASA, and it arrived at DFRC on 1 August 2001. The aircraft underwent an extensive modification program to equip it as a research aircraft mothership. However, instead of using the B-52H as a mothership for the atmospheric tests of the X-37 Space Maneuver Vehicle, NASA contracted that job to Scaled Composites and its White Knight aircraft. B-52H 61-0025 was retired in early 2006, having never flown a single research mission. It became a ground maintenance trainer for future B-52H crew chiefs with the 82nd Training Wing at Sheppard AFB.

The NB-52B carries the Pegasus booster and the X-43A No. 1 scramjet demonstrator. X-43A No. 1 was lost on 2 June 2001 when the Pegasus veered out of control after being dropped and igniting its rocket motor. (Tom Tschida / NASA Dryden Flight Research Center)

The X-43A is mounted on the front of the Pegasus booster. After the loss of X-43A No. 1, No. 2 and No. 3 went on to fly record-breaking missions. Also visible here are the camera fairing, observation bubble, and nose art of the NB-52B. (Tony Landis)

The X-43A was mounted on the front of the Pegasus booster. This photograph also shows the camera fairing, observation bubble, and nose art of the NB-52B. (Tony Landis / NASA Dryden Flight Research Center)

The launch panel operator (LPO) crew station in the NASA B-52H was in the right rear of the cockpit. A video monitor was located in front of the LPO. The LPO station included docking stations for two laptop computers for research vehicle command and monitoring functions. The test instrumentation engineer's video monitor is also partially visible at the right of the photograph. Between the two video monitors were the Fire Detection Panel and the Pylon Power Panel. (Author)

The NASA B-52H test instrumentation system consisted of various aircraft- and pylon-mounted sensors and signal-conditioning and data-recording equipment. All instrumentation parameters were available to be transmitted to the ground by a telemetry system. Sensor data was decommutated onboard the aircraft and displayed on a 17-inch video monitor at the test instrumentation engineer's station in the left rear of the cockpit. (Author)

To the left of the LPO (on the right side of the aircraft, since the LPO and test instrumentation engineer sit backward) were the system support power panel, launch control panel, and smoke system panel. The yellow ground emergency egress handle with black stripes was used to jettison the escape hatch over the seat. The LPO sat in the ejection seat used by the electronic warfare office on an operational B-52H. (Author)

The NASA B-52H could generate a smoke contrail to aid visual tracking. Smoke was generated by injecting Corvis oil into the exhaust stream of the No. 4 engine. The oil vaporized in the hot exhaust, creating the smoke. The smoke system consisted of a self-contained, removable pallet with two 100-gallon oil tanks, located in the aft portion of the weapons bay, and stainless steel plumbing from the weapons bay to the No. 4 engine. The smoke system was controlled from the LPO station using the smoke system panel. (Author)

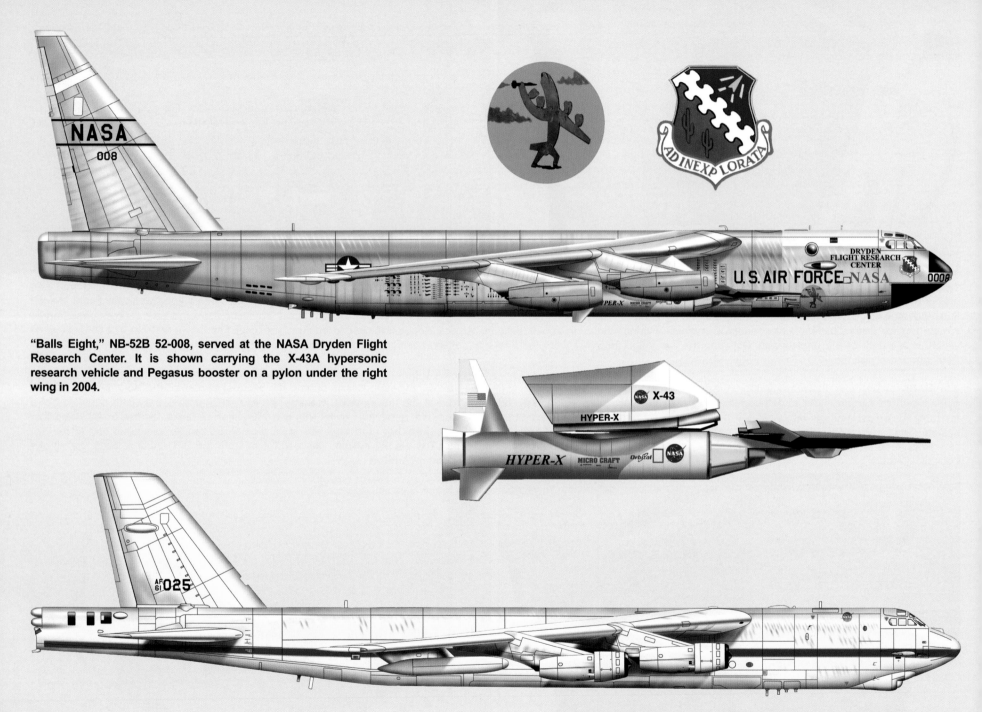

"Balls Eight," NB-52B 52-008, served at the NASA Dryden Flight Research Center. It is shown carrying the X-43A hypersonic research vehicle and Pegasus booster on a pylon under the right wing in 2004.

NASA received B-52H 61-0025 as a replacement for "Balls Eight" in 2001.

Even after the demise of the NASA B-52H program, the B-52 remained the mothership of choice for research vehicles.

Building on the success of the X-43A, the next step in advancing scramjet propulsion technology was to use hydrocarbon fuel instead of the hydrogen used by the X-43A. Hydrogen was used on the X-43A because it was the easiest fuel to use in a scramjet engine, but it was not an operationally practical fuel. The Defense Advanced Research Project Agency and the Air Force Research Laboratory sponsored and managed the X-51A project, with Boeing building the Waverider vehicle and Pratt & Whitney Rocketdyne building the SJY61 scramjet engine. The nearly wingless vehicle was named Waverider because it was designed to ride its own shockwave. As with the X-43A, key technical challenges for the X-51A included withstanding temperatures of 4000-5000 degree Celsius, maintaining combustion in a supersonic airflow inside the engine, and having the engine generate a positive net thrust.

The concept of operations for the X-51A provided for it to be launched from a B-52H. The launch was at 50,000 feet altitude, the edge of the envelope for the B-52H. After launch, a solid-propellant rocket booster accelerated the X-51A to high speed. At high speed, the scramjet was started and the X-51A would fly at hypersonic speeds, predicted to be Mach 6. Like the X-43A, the X-51A telemetered data during its flight and was not recovered.

The X-51A made its first captive carry flight on 9 December 2009. During a captive carry flight, the X-51A remained attached the wing of the B-52H and was not launched. The captive carry verified the high-altitude performance and handling qualities of the B-52H with the X-51A attached and tested communications and telemetry systems. B-52H 60-0050 launched the first X-51A on 26 May 2010. Although the vehicle was terminated early due to a communications problem caused by a hot gas leak, the mission was generally successful with the scramjet powering the flight for 143 seconds, compared to 11 seconds for X-43A #3.

X-51A #2 had an aborted launch in March 2011 when it failed to release from the B-52H. After redesigning the mechanism, B-52H 60-0031 launched X-51A #2 on 13 June 2011. The launch and rocket boost was successful, but the scramjet engine did not work properly for reasons that are still under investigation as this book was being written. Although a failure, learning from failures is one of the ways that research projects contribute to knowledge. The technology demonstrated by the X-51A may eventually be applied to hypersonic cruise missiles and air-breathing space boosters.

The X-51A stack consisted of a X-51A Waverider vehicle with a solid propellant rocket booster behind the X-51A. The stack was suspended from a heavily instrumented HSAB. This vehicle is X-51A #1. The booster is covered in a gray insulation blanket to maintain the propellant grain at the optimum temperature. The blanket was removed before flight. (Mike Cassidy / USAF)

B-52H 60-0050, the long-serving test aircraft assigned to the 419th Flight Test Squadron, launched X-51A #1 on 26 May 2010. The aircraft has its "Dragon's Inferno" nose art and below the "0050" retains the program emblem from an earlier flight test program for synthetic fuel. The crew launched the X-51A at 50,000 feet over the Point Mugu Naval Air Warfare Center Sea Range. (USAF)

The ground crew performs the final preparations on X-51A #2 prior to its flight. They have already removed the gray insulation blanket from the rocket booster. X-51A #2 could be visually distinguished from #1 because the white adapter between the booster and the research vehicle carried the inscription "In Dedication to Dae Hyun Kim." (Bob Ferguson / The Boeing Company)

B-52H 60-0031 launched X-51A #2. During this flight, the vehicle was successfully boosted to Mach 5 and started the scramjet engine, but did not reach full power. (Bob Ferguson / The Boeing Company)

X-51A #2 hangs suspended from the left wing of B-52H 60-0031. The nose and inlet of the X-51A were constructed of exotic metals to handle the tremendous temperatures created by flight at hypersonic speeds. The rest of the vehicle's bottom is covered with tiles of heat-resistant material. (Bob Ferguson / The Boeing Company)

Air Force Global Strike Command

Operations Enduring Freedom and Iraqi Freedom vindicated the assignment of the heavy bomber force to ACC, with the bombers successfully integrated into the full range of combat missions. But the capabilities in conventional and irregular warfare came at a cost. In a world where Russian and China were no longer enemies but remained nuclear armed nations of concern, and countries such as North Korea, Pakistan, Iran, and Syria either had nuclear weapons or were attempting to get them, the USAF nuclear mission remained. Unfortunately, the conventional focus led to a neglect of the nuclear role, which became apparent when the 5th BW had a nuclear weapons incident on 29-30 August 2007. AGM-129 missiles with live nuclear warheads were mistakenly loaded on a B-52H at Minot AFB and flown to Barksdale AFB. The nuclear warheads should have been removed before removing the missiles from storage, but the situation went undetected by maintenance and operations personnel at both bases. Numerous 2nd BW and 5th BW personnel were relieved, disciplined, or decertified as a result of this incident. In 2008, the 5th BW received an unsatisfactory rating on a Nuclear Surety Inspection and there was also a mistaken shipment of ballistic missile components to Taiwan. Among the casualties of the series of nuclear incidents were Secretary of the Air Force Michael W. Wynne and Chief of Staff General T. Michael Moseley, who were fired by Secretary of Defense Robert M. Gates.

As a result of these incidents, the USAF formed the Air Force Global Strike Command (AFGSC) to control all nuclear-capable bombers and ballistic missiles. Essentially a resurrection of SAC, AFGSC consisted of the 8th Air Force with the two B-52H and one B-2A wings (the B-1B was no longer nuclear-capable by this time and remained in ACC) and the 20th Air Force with the Minuteman III intercontinental ballistic missile wings. The 8th Air Force formally transferred from ACC to AFGSC on 1 February 2010. It was also designated as Task Force 204, providing nuclear bomber forces to US Strategic Command.

Sixty years after the first flight of the YB-52, the B-52H remains a cornerstone of American military power. As of 30 September 2011, the active B-52H fleet numbered 74, the survivors of 744 total B-52s that were built. Although engineers have calculated that the primary structure of the remaining aircraft should remain airworthy at current utilization rates through 2040, the continued viability of the B-52H as an operationally effective and logistically supportable weapon system depends on the funding of modernization programs. That funding is under pressure because of massive Federal deficits. But no matter what happens in the future, the B-52 has established itself as perhaps the most important American military aircraft since World War II, having a played a central role in the Cold War and every significant combat operations since it entered service. It is possible that the last B-52H crewmember has not yet been born, but even if the B-52H were retired today, it would be a legend.

B-52H 61-003 of the 69th BS, 5th BW departs Andersen AFB, Guam during the Valiant Shield 2010 exercise. The 69th BS was reactivated in 2009 and assigned to the 5th BW to give that wing two operational squadrons. Aircraft assigned to the 69th BS had a tail band with a red and black checkerboard and two yellow pinstripes (Airman 1st Class Jeffrey Schultze / USAF)

Forty-nine years after its delivery, B-52H 61-0036 of the 96th BS, 2nd BW remained part of America's first line strike force in 2011. Although intended to be replaced by the B-70, then by the B-1A, and then the B-2A, the B-52H has soldiered on. The combination of long range, heavy payload, and ability to be upgraded in avionics and weapons kept the B-52H relevant and effective far longer than could have been imaged when it entered service. (Kevin Cox / USAF)